alfred, lord tennyson

selected poems

SWEET
WATER
PRESS

alfred, lord tennyson
selected poems

Copyright © 2006 by Sweetwater Press

Produced by Cliff Road Books

ISBN: 1-58173-500-6
ISBN-13: 978-1-58173-500-0

Design by Pat Covert

Printed in China

Table of Contents

alfred, lord tennyson

selected poems

Claribel

Where Claribel low-lieth
  The breezes pause and die,
    Letting the rose-leaves fall;
But the solemn oak-tree sigheth,
    Thick-leaved, ambrosial,
  With an ancient melody
  Of an inward agony,
Where Claribel low-lieth.

At eve the beetle boometh
  Athwart the thicket lone;
At noon the wild bee hummeth
  About the moss'd headstone;
At midnight the moon cometh,
  And looketh down alone.
Her song the lintwhite swelleth,
The clear-voiced mavis dwelleth,
  The callow throstle lispeth,
The slumbrous wave outwelleth,
  The babbling runnel crispeth,
The hollow grot replieth
  Where Claribel low-lieth.

The Kraken

Below the thunders of the upper deep,
Far, far beneath in the abysmal sea,
His ancient, dreamless, uninvaded sleep
The Kraken sleepeth: faintest sunlights flee
About his shadowy sides; above him swell
Huge sponges of millenial growth and height;
And far away into the sickly light,
From many a wondrous grot and secret cell
Unnumber'ed and enormous polypi
Winnow with giant arms the slumbering green.
There hath he lain for ages, and will lie
Battening upon huge sea-worms in his sleep,
Until the latter fire shall heat the deep;
Then once by man and angels to be seen,
In roaring he shall rise and on the surface die.

Lilian

Airy, fairy Lilian,
Flitting, fairy Lilian,
When I ask her if she love me,
Claps her tiny hands above me,
Laughing all she can;
She'll not tell me if she love me,
Cruel little Lilian.

When my passion seeks
Pleasance in love-sighs,
She, looking thro' and thro' me
Thoroughly to undo me,
Smiling, never speaks:
So innocent-arch, so cunning-simple,
From beneath her gathered wimple
Glancing with black-beaded eyes,
Till the lightning laughters dimple
The baby-roses in her cheeks;
Then away she flies.

Prythee weep, May Lilian!
Gaiety without eclipse

Wearieth me, May Lilian;
Thro' my very heart it thrilleth
  When from crimson-threaded lips
Silver-treble laughter trilleth:
  Prythee weep, May Lilian!

IV

  Praying all I can,
If prayers will not hush thee,
    Airy Lilian,
Like a rose-leaf I will crush thee,
    Fairy Lilian.

Mariana

'Mariana in the moated grange.'

Measure for Measure

With blackest moss the flower-pots
    Were thickly crusted, one and all;
The rusted nails fell from the knots
    That held the pear to the gable-wall.
The broken sheds look'd sad and strange:
    Unlifted was the clinking latch;
    Weeded and worn the ancient thatch
Upon the lonely moated grange.
      She only said, 'My life is dreary,
        He cometh not,' she said;
      She said, 'I am aweary, aweary,
        I would that I were dead!'

Her tears fell with the dews at even;
    Her tears fell ere the dews were dried;
She could not look on the sweet heaven,
    Either at morn or eventide.
After the flitting of the bats,
    When thickest dark did trance the sky,
    She drew her casement-curtain by,
And glanced athwart the glooming flats.
      She only said, 'The night is dreary,
        He cometh not,' she said;
      She said, 'I am aweary, aweary,
        I would that I were dead!'

Upon the middle of the night,
    Waking she heard the night-fowl crow;
The cock sung out an hour ere light;
    From the dark fen the oxen's low
Came to her; without hope of change,
    In sleep she seem'd to walk forlorn,
    Till cold winds woke the gray-eyed morn
About the lonely moated grange.
        She only said, 'The day is dreary,
            He cometh not,' she said;
        She said, 'I am aweary, aweary,
            I would that I were dead!'

About a stone-cast from the wall
    A sluice with blacken'd waters slept,
And o'er it many, round and small,
    The cluster'd marish-mosses crept.
Hard by a poplar shook alway,
    All silver-green with gnarled bark:
    For leagues no other tree did mark
The level waste, the rounding gray.
        She only said, 'My life is dreary,
            He cometh not,' she said;
        She said, 'I am aweary, aweary,
            I would that I were dead!'

And ever when the moon was low,
    And the shrill winds were up and away,
In the white curtain, to and fro,
    She saw the gusty shadow sway.

But when the moon was very low,
    And wild winds bound within their cell,
    The shadow of the poplar fell
Upon her bed, across her brow.
        She only said, 'The night is dreary,
            He cometh not,' she said;
        She said, 'I am aweary, aweary,
            I would that I were dead!'

All day within the dreamy house,
    The doors upon their hinges creak'd;
The blue fly sung in the pane; the mouse
    Behind the mouldering wainscot shriek'd,
Or from the crevice peer'd about.
        Old faces glimmer'd thro' the doors,
        Old footsteps trod the upper floors,
Old voices call'd her from without.
        She only said, 'My life is dreary,
            He cometh not,' she said;
        She said, 'I am aweary, aweary,
            I would that I were dead!'

The sparrow's chirrup on the roof,
    The slow clock ticking, and the sound
Which to the wooing wind aloof
    The poplar made, did all confound
Her sense; but most she loathed the hour
        When the thick-moted sunbeam lay
        Athwart the chambers, and the day
Was sloping toward his western bower.

Then, said she, 'I am very dreary,
   He will not come,' she said;
She wept, 'I am aweary, aweary,
   O God, that I were dead!'

Ode to Memory

I

Thou who stealest fire,
From the fountains of the past,
To glorify the present, O, haste,
Visit my low desire!
Strengthen me, enlighten me!
I faint in this obscurity,
Thou dewy dawn of memory.

II

Come not as thou camest of late,
Flinging the gloom of yesternight
On the white day, but robed in soften'd light
Of orient state.
Whilome thou camest with the morning mist,
Even as a maid, whose stately brow
The dew-impearled winds of dawn have kiss'd,
When she, as thou,
Stays on her floating locks the lovely freight
Of overflowing blooms, and earliest shoots
Of orient green, giving safe pledge of fruits,
Which in wintertide shall star
The black earth with brilliance rare.

Whilome thou camest with the morning mist,
  And with the evening cloud,
Showering thy gleaned wealth into my open
      breast;
Those peerless flowers which in the rudest wind
      Never grow sere,
When rooted in the garden of the mind,
  Because they are the earliest of the year.
      Nor was the night thy shroud.
In sweet dreams softer than unbroken rest
Thou leddest by the hand thine infant Hope.
The eddying of her garments caught from thee
The light of thy great presence; and the cope
  Of the half-attain'd futurity,
  Tho' deep not fathomless,
Was cloven with the million stars which tremble
O'er the deep mind of dauntless infancy.
Small thought was there of life's distress;
For sure she deem'd no mist of earth could dull
Those spirit-thrilling eyes so keen and beautiful;
Sure she was nigher to heaven's spheres,
Listening the lordly music flowing from
      The illimitable years.
  O, strengthen me, enlighten me!
  I faint in this obscurity,
  Thou dewy dawn of memory.

IV

Come forth, I charge thee, arise,
Thou of the many tongues, the myriad eyes!
Thou comest not with shows of flaunting vines
     Unto mine inner eye,
     Divinest Memory!
  Thou wert not nursed by the waterfall
Which ever sounds and shines
  A pillar of white light upon the wall
Of purple cliffs, aloof descried:
Come from the woods that belt the gray hillside,
The seven elms, the poplars four
That stand beside my father's door,
And chiefly from the brook that loves
To purl o'er matted cress and ribbed sand,
Or dimple in the dark of rushy coves,
Drawing into his narrow earthen urn,
     In every elbow and turn,
The filter'd tribute of the rough woodland;
     O, hither lead thy feet!
Pour round mine ears the livelong bleat
Of the thick-fleeced sheep from wattled folds,
     Upon the ridged wolds,
When the first matin-song hath waken'd loud
Over the dark dewy earth forlorn,
What time the amber morn
Forth gushes from beneath a low-hung cloud.

Large dowries doth the raptured eye
  To the young spirit present
    When first she is wed,
      And like a bride of old,
    In triumph led,
        With music and sweet showers
        Of festal flowers,
  Unto the dwelling she must sway.
Well hast thou done, great artist Memory,
  In setting round thy first experiment
    With royal framework of wrought gold;
Needs must thou dearly love thy first essay,
And foremost in thy various gallery
  Place it, where sweetest sunlight falls
  Upon the storied walls;
        For the discovery

And newness of thine art so pleased thee
That all which thou hast drawn of fairest
Or boldest since but lightly weighs
With thee unto the love thou bearest
The first-born of thy genius. Artist-like,
Ever retiring thou dost gaze
On the prime labor of thine early days,
No matter what the sketch might be:
Whether the high field on the bushless pike,
Or even a sand-built ridge
Of heaped hills that mound the sea,

Overblown with murmurs harsh,
Or even a lowly cottage whence we see
Stretch'd wide and wild the waste enormous marsh,
Where from the frequent bridge,
Like emblems of infinity,
The trenched waters run from sky to sky;
Or a garden bower'd close
With plaited alleys of the trailing rose,
Long alleys falling down to twilight grots,
Or opening upon level plots
Of crowned lilies, standing near
Purple-spiked lavender:
Whither in after life retired
From brawling storms,
From weary wind,
With youthful fancy re-inspired,
We may hold converse with all forms
Of the many-sided mind,
And those whom passion hath not blinded,
Subtle-thoughted, myriad-minded.

My friend, with you to live alone
Were how much better than to own
A crown, a sceptre, and a throne!

O, strengthen me, englighten me!
I faint in this obscurity,
Thou dewy dawn of memory.

The Poet

The poet in a golden clime was born,
　　With golden stars above;
Dower'd with the hate of hate, the scorn of scorn,
　　　The love of love.

He saw thro' life and death, thro' good and ill,
　　He saw thro' his own soul.
The marvel of the everlasting will,
　　　An open scroll,

Before him lay; with echoing feet he threaded
　　The secretest walks of fame:
The viewless arrows of his thoughts were headed
　　　And wing'd with flame,

Like Indian reeds blown from his silver tongue,
　　And of so fierce a flight,
From Calpe unto Caucasus they sung,
　　　Filling with light

And vagrant melodies the winds which bore
　　Them earthward till they lit;
Then, like the arrow-seeds of the field flower,
　　　The fruitful wit

Cleaving took root, and springing forth anew
　　Where'er they fell, behold,
Like to the mother plant in semblance, grew
　　　A flower all gold,

And bravely furnish'd all abroad to fling
　　The winged shafts of truth,
To throng with stately blooms the breathing spring
　　　Of Hope and Youth.

So many minds did gird their orbs with beams,
　　Tho' one did fling the fire;
Heaven flow'd upon the soul in many dreams
　　　Of high desire.

Thus truth was multiplied on truth, the world
　　Like one great garden show'd,
And thro' the wreaths of floating dark up-curl'd,
　　Rare sunrise flow'd.

And Freedom rear'd in that august sunrise
　　Her beautiful bold brow,
When rites and forms before his burning eyes
　　　Melted like snow.

There was no blood upon her maiden robes
　　Sunn'd by those orient skies;
But round about the circles of the globes
　　　Of her keen eyes

And in her raiment's hem was traced in flame
　　WISDOM, a name to shake
All evil dreams of power–a sacred name.
　　　And when she spake,

Her words did gather thunder as they ran,
    And as the lightning to the thunder
Which follows it, riving the spirit of man,
    Making earth wonder,

So was their meaning to her words. No sword
    Of wrath her right arm whirl'd,
But one poor poet's scroll, and with *his* word
    She shook the world.

The Sea-Fairies

Slow sail'd the weary mariners and saw,
Betwixt the green brink and the running foam,
Sweet faces, rounded arms, and bosoms prest
To little harps of gold; and while they mused,
Whispering to each other half in fear,
Shrill music reach'd them on the middle sea.

Whither away, whither away, whither away? fly no
      more.
Whither away from the high green field, and the
      happy blossoming shore?
Day and night to the billow the fountain calls;
Down shower the gambolling waterfalls
From wandering over the lea;
Out of the live-green heart of the dells
They freshen the silvery-crimson shells,
And thick with white bells the clover-hill swells
High over the full-toned sea.
O, hither, come hither and furl your sails,
Come hither to me and to me;
Hither, come hither and frolic and play;
Here it is only the mew that wails;
We will sing to you all the day.
Mariner, mariner, furl your sails,
For here are the blissful downs and dales,
And merrily, merrily carol the gales,
And the spangle dances in bight and bay,
And the rainbow forms and flies on the land

Over the islands free;
And the rainbow lives in the curve of the sand;
Hither, come hither and see;
And the rainbow hangs on the poising wave,
And sweet is the color of cove and cave,
And sweet shall your welcome be.
O, hither, come hither, and be our lords,
For merry brides are we.
We will kiss sweet kisses, and speak sweet words;
O, listen, listen, your eyes shall glisten
With pleasure and love and jubilee.
O, listen, listen, your eyes shall glisten
When the sharp clear twang of the golden chords
Runs up the ridged sea.
Who can light on as happy a shore
All the world o'er, all the world o'er?
Whither away? listen and stay; mariner, mariner,
      fly no more.

The Deserted House

I

Life and Thought have gone away
    Side by side,
    Leaving door and windows wide;
Careless tenants they!

II

All within is dark as night:
In the windows is no light;
And no murmur at the door,
So frequent on its hinge before.

III

Close the door, the shutters close,
    Or thro' the windows we shall see
    The nakedness and vacancy
Of the dark deserted house.

IV

Come away; no more of mirth
    Is here or merry-making sound.
The house was builded of the earth,
    And shall fall again to ground.

V

Come away; for Life and Thought
 Here no longer dwell,
But in a city glorious—
A great and distant city—have bought
 A mansion incorruptible.
Would they could have stayed with us!

The Dying Swan

The plain was grassy, wild and bare,
Wide, wild, and open to the air,
Which had built up everywhere
    An under-roof of doleful gray.
With an inner voice the river ran,
Adown it floated a dying swan,
        And loudly did lament.
    It was the middle of the day.
Ever the weary wind went on,
        And took the reed-tops as it went.

Some blue peaks in the distance rose,
And white against the cold-white sky,
Shone out their crowning snows.
    One willow over the river wept,
And shook the wave as the wind did sigh;
Above in the wind was the swallow,
        Chasing itself at its own wild will,
        And far thro' the marish green and still
        The tangled water-courses slept,
Shot over with purple, and green, and yellow.

The wild swan's death-hymn took the soul
Of that waste place with joy
Hidden in sorrow. At first to the ear
The warble was low, and full and clear;
 And floating about the under-sky,
 Prevailing in weakness, the coronach stole
 Sometimes afar, and sometimes anear;
 But anon her awful jubilant voice,
 With a music strange and manifold,
Flow'd forth on a carol free and bold;
As when a mighty people rejoice
With shawms, and with cymbals, and harps of
   gold,
And the tumult of their acclaim is roll'd
Thro' the open gates of the city afar,
To the shepherd who watcheth the evening star.
And the creeping mosses and clambering weeds,
And the willow-branches hoar and dank,
And the wavy swell of the soughing reeds,
And the wave-worn horns of the echoing bank,
And the silvery marish-flowers that throng
The desolate creeks and pools among,
Were flooded over with eddying song.

The Mermaid

Who would be
A mermaid fair,
Singing alone,
Combing her hair
Under the sea,
In a golden curl
With a comb of pearl,
On a throne?

I would be a mermaid fair;
I would sing to myself the whole of the day;
With a comb of pearl I would comb my hair;
And still as I comb'd I would sing and say,
'Who is it loves me? who loves not me?'
I would comb my hair till my ringlets would fall
Low adown, low adown,
From under my starry sea-bud crown
Low adown and around,
And I should look like a fountain of gold
Springing alone
With a shrill inner sound,
Over the throne

In the midst of the hall;
Till that great sea-snake under the sea
From his coiled sleeps in the central deeps
Would slowly trail himself sevenfold
Round the hall where I sate, and look in at the
                gate
With his large calm eyes for the love of me.
And all the mermen under the sea
Would feel their immortality
Die in their hearts for the love of me.

III

But at night I would wander away, away,
    I would fling on each side my low-flowing locks,
And lightly vault from the throne and play
    With the mermen in and out of the rocks;
We would run to and fro, and hide and seek,
    On the broad sea-wolds in the crimson shells,
Whose silvery spikes are nighest the sea.
But if any came near I would call, and shriek,
And adown the steep like a wave I would leap
    From the diamond-ledges that jut from the dells;
For I would not be kiss'd by all who would list
Of the bold merry mermen under the sea.
They would sue me, and woo me, and flatter me,
In the purple twilights under the sea;
But the king of them all would carry me,
Woo me, and win me, and marry me,

In the branching jaspers under the sea.
Then all the dry-pied things that be
In the hueless mosses under the sea
Would curl round my silver feet silently,
All looking up for the love of me.
And if I should carol aloud, from aloft
All things that are forked, and horned, and soft
Would lean out from the hollow sphere of the sea,
All looking down for the love of me.

Morte d'Arthur

So all day long the noise of battle roll'd
Among the mountains by the winter sea,
Until King Arthur's table, man by man,
Had fallen in Lyonness about their lord,
King Arthur; then, because his wound was deep,
The bold Sir Bedivere uplifted him,
Sir Bedivere, the last of all his knights,
And bore him to a chapel nigh the field,
A broken chancel with a broken cross,
That stood on a dark strait of barren land.
On one side lay the ocean, and on one
Lay a great water, and the moon was full.
   Then spake King Arthur to Sir Bedivere:
'The sequel of to-day unsolders all
The goodliest fellowship of famous knights
Whereof this world holds record. Such a sleep
They sleep—the men I loved. I think that we
Shall never more, at any future time,
Delight our souls with talk of knightly deeds,
Walking about the gardens and the halls
Of Camelot, as in the days that were.
I perish by this people which I made,—
Tho' Merlin sware that I should come again
To rule once more—but let what will be be,
I am so deeply smitten thro' the helm
That without help I cannot last till morn.
Thou therefore take my brand Excalibur,
Which was my pride; for thou rememberest how

In those old days, one summer noon, an arm
Rose up from out the bosom of the lake,
Clothed in white samite, mystic, wonderful
Holding the sword—and how I row'd across
And took it, and have worn it, like a king
And, wheresoever I am sung or told
In aftertime, this also shall be known.
But now delay not; take Excalibur,
And fling him far into the middle mere;
Watch what thou seest, and lightly bring me
       word.'
  To him replied the bold Sir Bedivere:
'It is not meet, Sir King, to leave thee thus,
Aidless, alone, and smitten thro' the helm.
A little thing may harm a wounded man.
Yet I thy hest will all perform at full,
Watch what I see, and lightly bring thee word.'
  So saying, from the ruin'd shrine he stept
And in the moon athwart the place of tombs,
Where lay the mighty bones of ancient men,
Old knights, and over them the sea-wind sang
Shrill, chill, with flakes of foam. He, stepping
       down
By zigzag paths and juts of pointed rock,
Came on the shining levels of the lake.
  There drew he forth the brand Excalibur,
And o'er him, drawing it, the winter moon,
Brightening the skirts of a long cloud, ran forth
And sparkled keen with frost against the hilt;
For all the haft twinkled with diamond sparks,

Myriads of topaz-lights, and jacinth-work
Of subtlest jewellery. He gazed so long
That both his eyes were dazzled, as he stood,
This way and that dividing the swift mind,
In act to throw; but at the last it seem'd
Better to leave Excalibur conceal'd
There in the many-knotted water-flags,
That whistled stiff and dry about the marge.
So strode he back slow to the wounded king.

    Then spake King Arthur to Sir Bedivere:
'Hast thou perform'd my mission which I gave?
What is it thou hast seen, or what hast heard?'

    And answer made the bold Sir Bedivere:
'I heard the ripple washing in the reeds,
And the wild water lapping on the crag.'

    To whom replied King Arthur, faint and pale:
'Thou hast betray'd thy nature and thy name,
Not rendering true answer, as beseem'd
Thy fealty, nor like a noble knight;
For surer sign had follow'd, either hand,
Or voice, or else a motion of the mere.
This is a shameful thing for men to lie.
Yet now, I charge thee, quickly go again
As thou art lief and dear, and do the thing
I bade thee, watch, and lightly bring me word.'

    Then went Sir Bedivere the second time
Across the ridge, and paced beside the mere,
Counting the dewy pebbles, fix'd in thought;
But when he saw the wonder of the hilt,
How curiously and strangely chased, he smote

His palms together, and he cried aloud:
　　'And if indeed I cast the brand away,
Surely a precious thing, one worthy note,
Should thus be lost forever from the earth,
Which might have pleased the eyes of many men.
What good should follow this, if this were done?
What harm, undone? deep harm to disobey,
Seeing obedience is the bond of rule.
Were it well to obey then, if a king demand
An act unprofitable, against himself?
The king is sick, and knows not what he does.
What record, or what relic of my lord
Should be to aftertime, but empty breath
And rumors of a doubt? but were this kept,
Stored in some treasure-house of mighty kings,
Some one might show it at a joust of arms,
Saying, "King Arthur's sword, Excalibur,
Wrought by the lonely maiden of the lake;
Nine years she wrought it, sitting in the deeps
Upon the hidden bases of the hills."
So might some old man speak in the aftertime
To all the people, winning reverence;
But now much honor and much fame were lost.'

　　So spake he, clouded with his own conceit,
And hid Excalibur the second time,
And so strode back slow to the wounded king.
　　Then spoke King Arthur, breathing heavily:
'What is it thou hast seen? or what hast heard?'
　　And answer made the bold Sir Bedivere:
'I heard the water lapping on the crag,

And the long ripple washing in the reeds.'
   To whom replied King Arthur, much in wrath:
'Ah, miserable and unkind, untrue,
Unknightly, traitor-hearted! Woe is me!
Authority forgets a dying king,
Laid widow'd of the power in his eye
That bow'd the will. I see thee what thou art,
For thou, the latest-left of all my knights,
In whom should meet the offices of all,
Thou wouldst betray me for the precious hilt;
Either from lust of gold, or like a girl
Valuing the giddy pleasure of the eyes.
Yet, for a man may fail in duty twice,
And the third time may prosper, get thee hence;
But, if thou spare to fling Excalibur,
I will arise and slay thee with my hands.'
   Then quickly rose Sir Bedivere, and ran,
And, leaping down the ridges lightly, plunged
Among the bulrush-beds, and clutch'd the sword,
And strongly wheel'd and threw it. The great
          brand
Made lightnings in the splendor of the moon,
And flashing round and round, and whirl'd in an
          arch,
Shot like a streamer of the northern morn,
Seen where the moving isles of winter shock
By night, with noises of the northern sea.
So flash'd and fell the brand Excalibur;
But ere he dipt the surface, rose an arm
Cloth'd in white samite, mystic, wonderful,

And caught him by the hilt, and brandish'd him
Three times, and drew him under in the mere.
And lightly went the other to the king.

Then spoke King Arthur, drawing thicker breath:
'Now see I by thine eyes that this is done.
Speak out; what is it thou hast heard, or seen?'

And answer made the bold Sir Bedivere:
'Sir King, I closed mine eyelids, lest the gems
Should blind my purpose, for I never saw,
Nor shall see, here or elsewhere, till I die,
Not tho' I live three lives of mortal men,
So great a miracle as yonder hilt.
Then with both hands I flung him, wheeling him;
But when I look'd again, behold an arm,
Clothed in white samite, mystic, wonderful,
That caught him by the hilt, and brandish'd him
Three times, and drew him under in the mere.'

And answer made King Arthur, breathing hard:
'My end draws nigh; 'tis time that I were gone.
Make broad thy shoulders to receive my weight,
And bear me to the margin; yet I fear
My wound hath taken cold, and I shall die.'

So saying, from the pavement he half rose,
Slowly, with pain, reclining on his arm,
And looking wistfully with wide blue eyes
As in a picture. Him Sir Bedivere
Remorsefully regarded thro' his tears,
And would have spoken, but he found not words,
Then took with care, and kneeling on one knee,
O'er both his shoulders drew the languid hands,

And rising bore him thro' the place of tombs.
  But, as he walk'd, King Arthur panted hard,
Like one that feels a nightmare on his bed
When all the house is mute. So sigh'd the king,
Muttering and murmuring at his ear, 'Quick,
      quick!
I fear it is too late, and I shall die.'
But the other swiftly strode from ridge to ridge,
Clothed with his breath, and looking, as he
      walk'd,
Larger than human on the frozen hills.
He heard the deep behind him, and a cry
Before. His own thought drove him like a goad.
Dry clash'd his harness in the icy caves
And barren chasms, and all to left and right
The bare black cliff clang'd round him, as he
      based
His feet on juts of slippery crag that rang
Sharp-smitten with the dint of armed heels—
And on a sudden, lo! the level lake,
And the long glories of the winter moon.
  Then saw they how there hove a dusky barge,
Dark as a funeral scarf from stem to stern
Beneath them; and descending they were ware
That all the decks were dense with stately forms
Black-stoled, black-hooded, like a dream—by
      these
Three queens with crowns of gold—and from
      them rose
A cry that shiver'd to the tingling stars,

And, as it were one voice, an agony
Of lamentation, like a wind that shrills
All night in a waste land, where no one comes,
Or hath come, since the making of the world.
   Then murmur'd Arthur, 'Place me in the barge,'
And to the barge they came. There those three
            queens
Put forth their hands, and took the king, and
            wept.
But she that rose the tallest of them all
And fairest laid his head upon her lap,
And loosed the shatter'd casque, and chafed his
            hands,
And call'd him by his name, complaining loud,
And dropping bitter tears against his brow
Striped with dark blood; for all his face was white
And colorless, and like the wither'd moon
Smote by the fresh beam of the springing east;
And all his greaves and cuisses dash'd with drops
Of onset; and the light and lustrous curls—
That made his forehead like a rising sun
High from the dais-throne—were parch'd with
            dust;
Or, clotted into points and hanging loose,
Mix'd with the knightly growth that fringed his
            lips.
So like a shatter'd column lay the king;
Not like that Arthur who, with lance in rest,
From spur to plume a star of tournament,
Shot thro' the lists at Camelot, and charged

Before the eyes of ladies and of kings.
   Then loudly cried the bold Sir Bedivere:
'Ah! my Lord Arthur, whither shall I go?
Where shall I hide my forehead and my eyes?
For now I see the true old times are dead,
When every morning brought a noble chance,
And every chance brought out a noble knight.
Such times have been not since the light that led
The holy Elders with the gift of myrrh.
But now the whole ROUND TABLE is dissolved
Which was an image of the mighty world;
And I, the last, go forth companionless,
And the days darken round me, and the years,
Among new men, strange faces, other minds.'
   And slowly answer'd Arthur from the barge:
'The old order changeth, yielding place to new,
And God fulfils himself in many ways,
Lest one good custom should corrupt the world.
Comfort thyself: what comfort is in me?
I have lived my life, and that which I have done
May He within himself make pure! but thou,
If thou shouldst never see my face again,
Pray for my soul. More things are wrought by
            prayer
Than this world dreams of. Wherefore, let thy
            voice
Rise like a fountain for me night and day.
For what are men better than sheep or goats
That nourish a blind life within the brain,
If, knowing God, they lift not hands of prayer

Both for themselves and those who call them
    friend?
For so the whole round earth is every way
Bound by gold chains about the feet of God.
But now farewell. I am going a long way
With these thou seest—if indeed I go—
For all my mind is clouded with a doubt—
To the island-valley of Avilion;
Where falls not hail, or rain, or any snow,
Nor ever wind blows loudly, but it lies
Deep-meadow'd, happy, fair with orchard lawns
And bowery hollows crown'd with summer sea,
Where I will heal me of my grievous wound.'
  So said he, and the barge with oar and sail
Moved from the brink, like some full-breasted
    swan
That, fluting a wild carol ere her death,
Ruffles her pure cold plume, and takes the flood
With swarthy webs. Long stood Sir Bedivere
Revolving many memories, till the hull
Look'd one black dot against the verge of dawn,
And on the mere the wailing died away.

The Lady of Shalott

Part I

On either side the river lie
Long fields of barley and of rye,
That clothe the wold and meet the sky;
And thro' the field the road runs by
    To many-tower'd Camelot;
And up and down the people go,
Gazing where the lilies blow
Round an island there below,
    The island of Shalott.

Willows whiten, aspens quiver,
Little breezes dusk and shiver
Thro' the wave that runs for ever
By the island in the river
    Flowing down to Camelot.
Four gray walls, and four gray towers,
Overlook a space of flowers,
And the silent isle imbowers
    The Lady of Shalott.

By the margin, willow-veil'd,
Slide the heavy barges trail'd
By slow horses; and unhail'd
The shallop flitteth silken-sail'd
    Skimming down to Camelot:
But who hath seen her wave her hand?

Or at the casement seen her stand?
Or is she known in all the land,
    The Lady of Shalott?

Only reapers, reaping early
In among the bearded barley,
Hear a song that echoes cheerly
From the river winding clearly,
    Down to tower'd Camelot:
And by the moon the reaper weary,
Piling sheaves in uplands airy,
Listening, whispers "Tis the fairy
    Lady of Shalott.'

Part II

There she weaves by night and day
A magic web with colors gay.
She has heard a whisper say,
A curse is on her if she stay
    To look down to Camelot.
She knows not what the curse may be,
And so she weaveth steadily,
And little other care hath she,
    The Lady of Shalott.

And moving thro' a mirror clear
That hangs before her all the year,
Shadows of the world appear.
There she sees the highway near

Winding down to Camelot;
There the river eddy whirls,
And there the surly village-churls,
And the red cloaks of market girls,
        Pass onward from Shalott.

Sometimes a troop of damsels glad,
An abbot on an ambling pad,
Sometimes a curly shepherd-lad,
Or long-hair'd page in crimson clad,
        Goes by to tower'd Camelot;
And sometimes thro' the mirror blue
The knights come riding two and two:
She hath no loyal knight and true,
        The Lady of Shalott.

But in her web she still delights
To weave the mirror's magic sights,
For often thro' the silent nights
A funeral, with plumes and lights
        And music, went to Camelot;
Or when the moon was overhead,
Came two young lovers lately wed;
'I am half sick of shadows,' said
        The Lady of Shalott.

Part III

A bow-shot from her bower-eaves,
He rode between the barley-sheaves,

44

The sun came dazzling thro' the leaves,
And flamed upon the brazen greaves
    Of bold Sir Lancelot.
A red-cross knight for ever kneel'd
To a lady in his shield,
That sparkled on the yellow field,
    Beside remote Shalott.

The gemmy bridle glitter'd free,
Like to some branch of stars we see
Hung in the golden Galaxy.
The bridle bells rang merrily
    As he rode down to Camelot;
And from his blazon'd baldric slung
A mighty silver bugle hung,
And as he rode his armor rung,
    Beside remote Shalott.

All in the blue unclouded weather
Thick-jewelled shone the saddle-leather,
The helmet and the helmet-feather
Burn'd like one burning flame together,
    As he rode down to Camelot.
As often thro' the purple night,
Below the starry clusters bright,
Some bearded meteor, trailing light,
    Moves over still Shalott.

His broad clear brow in sunlight glow'd;
On burnish'd hooves his war-horse trode;

From underneath his helmet flow'd
His coal-black curls as on he rode,
    As he rode down to Camelot.
From the bank and from the river
He flash'd into the crystal mirror,
'Tirra lirra,' by the river
    Sang Sir Lancelot.

She left the web, she left the loom,
She made three paces thro' the room,
She saw the water-lily bloom,
She saw the helmet and the plume,
    She look'd down to Camelot.
Out flew the web and floated wide;
The mirror crack'd from side to side;
'The curse is come upon me,' cried
    The Lady of Shalott.

Part IV

In the stormy east-wind straining,
The pale yellow woods were waning,
The broad stream in his banks complaining,
Heavily the low sky raining
    Over tower'd Camelot;
Down she came and found a boat
Beneath a willow left afloat,
And round about the prow she wrote
    The Lady of Shalott.

And down the river's dim expanse
Like some bold seër in a trance,
Seeing all his own mischance—
With a glassy countenance
    Did she look to Camelot.
And at the closing of the day
She loosed the chain, and down she lay;
The broad stream bore her far away,
    The Lady of Shalott.

Lying, robed in snowy white
That loosely flew to left and right—
The leaves upon her falling light—
Thro' the noises of the night
    She floated down to Camelot;
And as the boat-head wound along
The willowy hills and fields among,
They heard her singing her last song,
    The Lady of Shalott.

Heard a carol, mournful, holy,
Chanted loudly, chanted lowly,
Till her blood was frozen slowly,
And her eyes were darken'd wholly,
    Turn'd to tower'd Camelot.
For ere she reach'd upon the tide
The first house by the water-side,
Singing in her song she died,
    The Lady of Shalott.

Under tower and balcony,
By garden-wall and gallery,
A gleaming shape she floated by,
Dead-pale between the houses high,
    Silent into Camelot.
Out upon the wharfs they came,
Knight and burgher, lord and dame,
And round the prow they read her name,
    The Lady of Shalott.

Who is this? and what is here?
And in the lighted palace near
Died the sound of royal cheer;
And they cross'd themselves for fear,
    All the knights at Camelot:
But Lancelot mused a little space;
He said, 'She has a lovely face;
God in his mercy lend her grace,
    The Lady of Shalott.'

The Palace of Art

I built my soul a lordly pleasure-house,
   Wherein at ease for aye to dwell.
I said, 'O Soul, make merry and carouse,
     Dear soul, for all is well.'

A huge crag-platform, smooth as burnish'd brass,
   I chose. The ranged ramparts bright
From level meadow-bases of deep grass
     Suddenly scaled the light.

Thereon I built it firm. Of ledge or shelf
   The rock rose clear, or winding stair.
My soul would live alone unto herself
     In her high palace there.

And 'while the world runs round and round,' I
        said,
   'Reign thou apart, a quiet king,
Still as, while Saturn whirls, his steadfast shade
     Sleeps on his luminous ring.'

To which my soul made answer readily:
   'Trust me, in bliss I shall abide
In this great mansion, that is built for me,
     So royal-rich and wide.'

—————————

Four courts I made, East, West and South and
        North,
  In each a squared lawn, wherefrom
The golden gorge of dragons spouted forth
    A flood of fountain-foam.

And round the cool green courts there ran a row
  Of cloisters, branch'd like mighty woods,
Echoing all night to that sonorous flow
    Of spouted fountain-floods;

And round the roofs a gilded gallery
  That lent broad verge to distant lands,
Far as the wild swan wings, to where the sky
    Dipt down to sea and sands.

From those four jets four currents in one swell
  Across the mountain stream'd below
In misty folds, that floating as they fell
    Lit up a torrent-bow.

And high on every peak a statue seem'd
  To hang on tiptoe, tossing up
A cloud of incense of all odor steam'd
    From out a golden cup.

So that she thought, 'And who shall gaze upon
  My palace with unblinded eyes,
While this great bow will waver in the sun,
    And that sweet incense rise?'

For that sweet incense rose and never fail'd,
   And, while day sank or mounted higher,
The light aerial gallery, golden-rail'd,
    Burnt like a fringe of fire.

Likewise the deep-set windows, stain'd and traced,
   Would seem slow-flaming crimson fires
From shadow'd grots of arches interlaced,
    And tipt with frost-like spires.

Full of long-sounding corridors it was,
   That over-vaulted grateful gloom,
Thro' which the livelong day my soul did pass,
    Well-pleased, from room to room.

Full of great rooms and small the palace stood,
   All various, each a perfect whole
From living Nature, fit for every mood
    And change of my still soul.

For some were hung with arras green and blue,
   Showing a gaudy summer-morn,
Where with puff'd cheek the belted hunter blew
    His wreathed bugle-horn.

One seem'd all dark and red—a tract of sand,
   And some one pacing there alone,
Who paced for ever in a glimmering land,
    Lit with a low large moon.

One show'd an iron coast and angry waves.
　You seem'd to hear them climb and fall
And roar rock-thwarted under bellowing caves,
　　Beneath the windy wall.

And one, a full-fed river winding slow
　By herds upon an endless plain,
The ragged rims of thunder brooding low,
　　With shadow-streaks of rain.

And one, the reapers at their sultry toil.
　In front they bound the sheaves. Behind
Were realms of upland, prodigal in oil,
　　And hoary to the wind.

And one a foreground black with stones and slags;
　Beyond, a line of heights; and higher
All barr'd with long white cloud the scornful crags;
　　And highest, snow and fire.

And one, an English home—gray twilight pour'd
　On dewy pastures, dewy trees,
Softer than sleep—all things in order stored,
　　A haunt of ancient Peace.

Nor these alone, but every landscape fair,
　As fit for every mood of mind,
Or gay, or grave, or sweet, or stern, was there,
　　Not less than truth design'd.

Or the maid-mother by a crucifix,
    In tracts of pasture sunny-warm,
Beneath branch-work of costly sardonyx
        Sat smiling, babe in arm.

Or in a clear-wall'd city on the sea,
    Near gilded organ-pipes, her hair
Wound with white roses, slept Saint Cecily;
        An angel look'd at her.

Or thronging all one porch of Paradise
    A group of Houris bow'd to see
The dying Islamite, with hands and eyes
        That said, We wait for thee.

Or mythic Uther's deeply-wounded son
    In some fair space of sloping greens
Lay, dozing in the vale of Avalon,
        And watch'd by weeping queens.

Or hollowing one hand against his ear,
    To list a foot-fall, ere he saw
The wood-nymph, stay'd the Ausonian king to hear
        Of wisdom and of law.

Or over hills with peaky tops engrail'd,
    And many a tract of palm and rice,
The throne of Indian Cama slowly sail'd
        A summer fann'd with spice.

Or sweet Europa's mantle blew unclasp'd,
    From off her shoulder backward borne;
From one hand droop'd a crocus; one hand
        grasp'd
    The mild bull's golden horn.

Or else flush'd Ganymede, his rosy thigh
    Half-buried in the eagle's down,
Sole as a flying star shot thro' the sky
    Above the pillar'd town.

Nor these alone; but every legend fair
    Which the supreme Caucasian mind
Carved out of Nature for itself was there,
    Not less than life design'd.

———————————

Then in the towers I placed great bells that swung,
    Moved of themselves, with silver sound;
And with choice paintings of wise men I hung
    The royal dais round.

For there was Milton like a seraph strong,
    Beside him Shakespeare bland and mild;
And there the world-worn Dante grasp'd his song,
    And somewhat grimly smiled.

And there the Ionian father of the rest;
    A million wrinkles carved his skin;

A hundred winters snow'd upon his breast,
    From cheek and throat and chin.

Above, the fair hall-ceiling stately-set
    Many an arch high up did lift,
And angels rising and descending met
    With interchange of gift.

Below was all mosaic choicely plann'd
    With cycles of the human tale
Of this wide world, the times of every land
    So wrought they will not fail.

The people here, a beast of burden slow,
    Toil'd onward, prick'd with goads and stings;
Here play'd, a tiger, rolling to and fro
    The heads and crowns of kings;

Here rose, an athlete, strong to break or bind
    All force in bonds that might endure,
And here once more like some sick man declined,
    And trusted any cure.

But over these she trod; and those great bells
    Began to chime. She took her throne;
She sat betwixt the shining oriels,
    To sing her songs alone.

And thro' the topmost oriels' colored flame
    Two godlike faces gazed below;

Plato the wise, and large-brow'd Verulam,
    The first of those who know.

And all those names, that in their motion were
    Full-welling fountain-heads of change,
Betwixt the slender shafts were blazon'd fair
    In diverse raiment strange;

Thro' which the lights, rose, amber, emerald, blue,
    Flush'd in her temples and her eyes,
And from her lips, as morn from Memnon, drew
    Rivers of melodies.

No nightingale delighteth to prolong
    Her low preamble all alone,
More than my soul to hear her echo'd song
    Throb thro' the ribbed stone;

Singing and murmuring in her feastful mirth,
    Joying to feel herself alive,
Lord over Nature, lord of the visible earth,
    Lord of the senses five;

Communing with herself: 'All these are mine,
    And let the world have peace or wars,
'Tis one to me.' She—when young night divine
    Crown'd dying day with stars,

Making sweet close of his delicious toils—
    Lit light in wreaths and anadems,

And pure quintessences of precious oils
    In hallow'd moons of gems,

To mimic heaven; and clapt her hands and cried,
   'I marvel if my still delight
In this great house so royal-rich and wide
    Be flatter'd to the height.

'O all things fair to sate my various eyes!
   O shapes and hues that please me well!
O silent faces of the Great and Wise,
    My Gods, with whom I dwell!

'O Godlike isolation which art mine,
   I can but count thee perfect gain,
What time I watch the darkening droves of swine
    That range on yonder plain.

'In filthy sloughs they roll a prurient skin,
   They graze and wallow, breed and sleep;
And oft some brainless devil enters in,
    And drives them to the deep.'

Then of the moral instinct would she prate
   And of the rising from the dead,
As hers by right of full-accomplish'd Fate;
    And at the last she said:

'I take possession of man's mind and deed.
   I care not what the sects may brawl.

I sit as God holding no form of creed,
    But contemplating all.'

———————————

Full oft the riddle of the painful earth
   Flash'd thro' her as she sat alone,
Yet not the less held she her solemn mirth,
    And intellectual throne.

And so she throve and prosper'd; so three years
   She prosper'd; on the fourth she fell,
Like Herod, when the shout was in his ears,
    Struck thro' with pangs of hell.

Lest she should fail and perish utterly,
   God, before whom ever lie bare
The abysmal deeps of personality,
    Plagued her with sore despair.

When she would think, where'er she turn'd her
        sight
   The airy hand confusion wrought,
Wrote, 'Mene, mene,' and divided quite
    The kingdom of her thought.

Deep dread and loathing of her solitude
   Fell on her, from which mood was born
Scorn of herself; again, from out that mood
    Laughter at her self-scorn.

'What! is not this my place of strength,' she said,
    'My spacious mansion built for me,
Whereof the strong foundation-stones were laid
      Since my first memory?'

But in dark corners of her palace stood
    Uncertain shapes; and unawares
On white-eyed phantasms weeping tears of blood,
      And horrible nightmares,

And hollow shades enclosing hearts of flame,
    And, with dim fretted foreheads all,
On corpses three-months-old at noon she came,
      That stood against the wall.

A spot of dull stagnation, without light
    Or power of movement, seem'd my soul,
Mid onward-sloping motions infinite
      Making for one sure goal;

A still salt pool, lock'd in with bars of sand,
    Left on the shore, that hears all night
The plunging seas draw backward from the land
      Their moon-led waters white;

A star that with the choral starry dance
    Join'd not, but stood, and standing saw
The hollow orb of moving Circumstance
      Roll'd round by one fix'd law.

Back on herself her serpent pride had curl'd.
  'No voice,' she shriek'd in that lone hall,
'No voice breaks thro' the stillness of this world;
    One deep, deep silence all!'

She, mouldering with the dull earth's mouldering
        sod,
  Inwrapt tenfold in slothful shame,
Lay there exiled from eternal God,
    Lost to her place and name;

And death and life she hated equally,
  And nothing saw, for her despair,
But dreadful time, dreadful eternity,
    No comfort anywhere;

Remaining utterly confused with fears,
  And ever worse with growing time,
And ever unrelieved by dismal tears,
    And all alone in crime.

Shut up as in a crumbling tomb, girt round
  With blackness as a solid wall,
Far off she seem'd to hear the dully sound
    Of human footsteps fall:

As in strange lands a traveller walking slow,
  In doubt and great perplexity,
A little before moonrise hears the low
    Moan of an unknown sea;

And knows not if it be thunder, or a sound
    Of rocks thrown down, or one deep cry
Of great wild beasts; then thinketh, 'I have found
        A new land, but I die.'

She howl'd aloud, 'I am on fire within.
    There comes no murmur of reply.
What is it that will take away my sin,
        And save me lest I die?'

So when four years were wholly finished,
    She threw her royal robes away.
'Make me a cottage in the vale,' she said,
        'Where I may mourn and pray.

'Yet pull not down my palace towers, that are
    So lightly, beautifully built;
Perchance I may return with others there
        When I have purged my guilt.'

The Lotos-Eaters

'Courage!' he said, and pointed toward the land,
'This mounting wave will roll us shoreward soon.'
In the afternoon they came unto a land
In which it seemed always afternoon.
All round the coast the languid air did swoon,
Breathing like one that hath a weary dream.
Full-faced above the valley stood the moon;
And, like a downward smoke, the slender stream
Along the cliff to fall and pause and fall did seem.

A land of streams! some, like a downward smoke,
Slow-dropping veils of thinnest lawn, did go;
And some thro' wavering lights and shadows
        broke,
Rolling a slumbrous sheet of foam below.
They saw the gleaming river seaward flow
From the inner land; far off, three mountain-tops,
Three silent pinnacles of aged snow,
Stood sunset-flush'd: and dew'd with showery
        drops,
Up-clomb the shadowy pine above the woven
        copse.

The charmed sunset linger'd low adown
In the red West; thro' mountain clefts the dale
Was seen far inland, and the yellow down
Border'd with palm, and many a winding vale
And meadow, set with slender galingale;

A land where all things always seem'd the same!
And round about the keel with faces pale,
Dark faces pale against that rosy flame,
The mild-eyed melancholy Lotos-eaters came.

Branches they bore of that enchanted stem,
Laden with flower and fruit, whereof they gave
To each, but whoso did receive of them
And taste, to him the gushing of the wave
Far far away did seem to mourn and rave
On alien shores; and if his fellow spake,
His voice was thin, as voices from the grave;
And deep-asleep he seem'd, yet all awake,
And music in his ears his beating heart did make.

They sat them down upon the yellow sand,
Between the sun and the moon upon the shore;
And sweet it was to dream of Fatherland,
Of child, and wife, and slave; but evermore
Most weary seem'd the sea, weary the oar,
Weary the wandering fields of barren foam.
Then some one said, 'We will return no more;'
And all at once they sang, 'Our island home
Is far beyond the wave; we will no longer roam.'

Saint Simeon Stylites

Altho' I be the basest of mankind,
From scalp to sole one slough and crust of sin,
Unfit for earth, unfit for heaven, scarce meet
For troops of devils, mad with blasphemy,
I will not cease to grasp the hope I hold
Of saintdom, and to clamor, mourn, and sob,
Battering the gates of heaven with storms of
        prayer,
Have mercy, Lord, and take away my sin!
  Let this avail, just, dreadful, mighty God,
This not be all in vain that thrice ten years,
Thrice multiplied by superhuman pangs,
In hungers and in thirsts, fevers and cold,
In coughs, aches, stitches, ulcerous throes and
        cramps,
A sign betwixt the meadow and the cloud,
Patient on this tall pillar I have borne
Rain, wind, frost, heat, hail, damp, and sleet, and
        snow;
And I had hoped that ere this period closed
Thou wouldst have caught me up into thy rest,
Denying not these weather-beaten limbs
The meed of saints, the white robe and the palm.
  O, take the meaning, Lord! I do not breathe,
Not whisper, any murmur of complaint.
Pain heap'd ten-hundred-fold to this, were still
Less burthen, by ten-hundred-fold, to bear,
Than were those lead-like tons of sin that crush'd

My spirit flat before thee.

       O Lord, Lord,
Thou knowest I bore this better at the first,
For I was strong and hale of body then;
And tho' my teeth, which now are dropt away,
Would chatter with the cold, and all my beard
Was tagg'd with icy fringes in the moon,
I drown'd the whoopings of the owl with sound
Of pious hymns and psalms, and sometimes saw
An angel stand and watch me, as I sang.
Now am I feeble grown; my end draws nigh.
I hope my end draws nigh: half deaf I am,
So that I scarce can hear the people hum
About the column's base, and almost blind,
And scarce can recognize the fields I know;
And both my thighs are rotted with the dew;
Yet cease I not to clamor and to cry,
While my stiff spine can hold my weary head,
Till all my limbs drop piecemeal from the stone,
Have mercy, mercy! take away my sin!

 O Jesus, if thou wilt not save my soul,
Who may be saved? who is it may be saved?
Who may be made a saint if I fail here?
Show me the man hath suffer'd more than I.
For did not all thy martyrs die one death?
For either they were stoned, or crucified,
Or burn'd in fire, or boil'd in oil, or sawn
In twain beneath the ribs; but I die here
To-day, and whole years long, a life of death.
Bear witness, if I could have found a way—

And heedfully I sifted all my thought—
More slowly-painful to subdue this home
Of sin, my flesh, which I despise and hate,
I had not stinted practice, O my God!
  For not alone this pillar-punishment,
Not this alone I bore; but while I lived
In the white convent down the valley there,
For many weeks about my loins I wore
The rope that haled the buckets from the well,
Twisted as tight as I could knot the noose;
And spake not of it to a single soul,
Until the ulcer, eating thro' my skin,
Betray'd my secret penance, so that all
My brethren marvell'd greatly. More than this
I bore, whereof, O God, thou knowest all.
  Three winters, that my soul might grow to thee,
I lived up there on yonder mountain-side.
My right leg chain'd into the crag, I lay
Pent in a roofless close of ragged stones;
Inswathed sometimes in wandering mist, and twice
Black'd with thy branding thunder, and sometimes
Sucking the damps for drink, and eating not,
Except the spare chance-gift of those that came
To touch my body and be heal'd, and live.
And they say then that I work'd miracles,
Whereof my fame is loud amongst mankind,
Cured lameness, palsies, cancers. Thou, O God,
Knowest alone whether this was or no.
Have mercy, mercy! cover all my sin!
  Then, that I might be more alone with thee,

Three years I lived upon a pillar, high
Six cubits, and three years on one of twelve;
And twice three years I crouch'd on one that rose
Twenty by measure; last of all, I grew
Twice ten long weary, weary years to this,
That numbers forty cubits from the soil.

   I think that I have borne as much as this—
Or else I dream—and for so long a time,
If I may measure time by yon slow light,
And this high dial, which my sorrow crowns—
So much—even so.

                            And yet I know not well,
For that the evil ones come here, and say,
'Fall down, O Simeon; thou hast suffer'd long
For ages and for ages!' then they prate
Of penances I cannot have gone thro',
Perplexing me with lies; and oft I fall,
Maybe for months, in such blind lethargies
That Heaven, and Earth, and Time are choked.

                            But yet
Bethink thee, Lord, while thou and all the saints
Enjoy themselves in heaven, and men on earth
House in the shade of comfortable roofs,
Sit with their wives by fires, eat wholesome food,
And wear warm clothes, and even beasts have stalls,
I, 'tween the spring and downfall of the light,
Bow down one thousand and two hundred times,
To Christ, the Virgin Mother, and the saints;
Or in the night, after a little sleep,
I wake; the chill stars sparkle; I am wet

With drenching dews, or stiff with crackling frost.
I wear an undressed goatskin on my back;
A grazing iron collar grinds my neck;
And in my weak, lean arms I lift the cross,
And strive and wrestle with thee till I die.
O, mercy, mercy! wash away my sin!

   O Lord, thou knowest what a man I am;
A sinful man, conceived and born in sin.
'Tis their own doing; this is none of mine;
Lay it not to me. Am I to blame for this,
That here come those that worship me? Ha! ha!
They think that I am somewhat. What am I?
The silly people take me for a saint,
And bring me offerings of fruit and flowers;
And I, in truth—thou wilt bear witness here—
Have all in all endured as much, and more,
Than many just and holy men, whose names
Are register'd and calendar'd for saints.

   Good people, you do ill to kneel to me.
What is it I can have done to merit this?
I am a sinner viler than you all.
It may be I have wrought some miracles,
And cured some halt and maim'd; but what of
        that?
It may be no one, even among the saints,
May match his pains with mine; but what of that?
Yet do not rise; for you may look on me,
And in your looking you may kneel to God.
Speak! is there any of you halt or maim'd?
I think you know I have some power with Heaven

From my long penance; let him speak his wish.

   Yes, I can heal him. Power goes forth from me.
They say that they are heal'd. Ah, hark! they shout
'Saint Simeon Stylites.' Why, if so,
God reaps a harvest in me. O my soul,
God reaps a harvest in thee! If this be,
Can I work miracles and not be saved?
This is not told of any. They were saints.
It cannot be but that I shall be saved,
Yea, crown'd a saint. They shout, 'Behold a saint!'
And lower voices saint me from above.
Courage, Saint Simeon! This dull chrysalis
Cracks into shining wings, and hope ere death
Spreads more and more and more, that God hath
      now
Sponged and made blank of crimeful record all
My mortal archives.

           O my sons, my sons,
I, Simeon of the pillar, by surname
Stylites, among men; I, Simeon,
The watcher on the column till the end;
I, Simeon, whose brain the sunshine bakes;
I, whose bald brows in silent hours become
Unnaturally hoar with rime, do now
From my high nest of penance here proclaim
That Pontius and Iscariot by my side
Show'd like fair seraphs. On the coals I lay,
A vessel full of sin; all hell beneath
Made me boil over. Devils pluck'd my sleeve,
Abaddon and Asmodeus caught at me.

I smote them with the cross; they swarm'd again.
In bed like monstrous apes they crush'd my chest;
They flapp'd my light out as I read; I saw
Their faces grow between me and my book;
With coltlike whinny and with hoggish whine
They burst my prayer. Yet this way was left,
And by this way I 'scaped them. Mortify
Your flesh, like me, with scourges and with thorns;
Smite, shrink not, spare not. If it may be, fast
Whole Lents, and pray. I hardly, with slow steps,
With slow, faint steps, and much exceeding pain,
Have scrambled past those pits of fire, that still
Sing in mine ears. But yield not me the praise;
God only thro' his bounty hath thought fit,
Among the powers and princes of this world,
To make me an example to mankind,
Which few can reach to. Yet I do not say
But that a time may come—yea, even now,
Now, now, his footsteps smite the threshold stairs
Of life—I say, that time is at the doors
When you may worship me without reproach;
For I will leave my relics in your land,
And you may carve a shrine about my dust,
And burn a fragrant lamp before my bones,
When I am gather'd to the glorious saints.

While I spake then, a sting of shrewdest pain
Ran shrivelling thro' me, and a cloudlike change,
In passing, with a grosser film made thick
These heavy, horny eyes. The end! the end!
Surely the end! What's here? a shape, a shade,

A flash of light. Is that the angel there
That holds a crown? Come blessed brother, come!
I know thy glittering face. I waited long;
My brows are ready. What! deny it now?
Nay, draw, draw, draw nigh. So I clutch it. Christ!
'Tis gone; 'tis here again; the crown! the crown!
So now 'tis fitted on and grows to me,
And from it melt the dews of Paradise,
Sweet! sweet! spikenard, and balm, and
        frankincense.
Ah! let me not be fool'd, sweet saints; I trust
That I am whole, and clean, and meet for Heaven.
  Speak, if there be a priest, a man of God,
Among you there, and let him presently
Approach, and lean a ladder on the shaft,
And climbing up into my airy home,
Deliver me the blessed sacrament;
For by the warning of the Holy Ghost,
I prophesy that I shall die to-night,
A quarter before twelve.
                But thou, O Lord,
Aid all this foolish people; let them take
Example, pattern; lead them to thy light.

Ulysses

It little profits that an idle king,
By this still hearth, among these barren crags,
Matched with an aged wife, I mete and dole
Unequal laws unto a savage race,
That hoard, and sleep, and feed, and know not
      me.
I cannot rest from travel; I will drink
Life to the lees. All times I have enjoy'd
Greatly, have suffer'd greatly, both with those
That loved me, and alone; on shore, and when
Thro' scudding drifts the rainy Hyades
Vext the dim sea. I am become a name;
For always roaming with a hungry heart
Much have I seen and known,—cities of men
And manners, climates, councils, governments,
Myself not least, but honor'd of them all,—
And drunk delight of battle with my peers,
Far on the ringing plains of windy Troy.
I am a part of all that I have met;
Yet all experience is an arch wherethro'
Gleams that untravel'd world whose margin fades
For ever and for ever when I move.
How dull it is to pause, to make an end,
To rust unburnish'd, not to shine in use!
As tho' to breathe were life! Life piled on life
Were all too little, and of one to me
Little remains; but every hour is saved
From that eternal silence, something more,

A bringer of new things; and vile it were
For some three suns to store and hoard myself,
And this gray spirit yearning in desire
To follow knowledge like a sinking star,
Beyond the utmost bound of human thought.

    This is my son, mine own Telemachus,
To whom I leave the sceptre and the isle,—
Well-loved of me, discerning to fulfill
This labor, by slow prudence to make mild
A rugged people, and thro' soft degrees
Subdue them to the useful and the good.
Most blameless is he, centred in the sphere
Of common duties, decent not to fail
In offices of tenderness, and pay
Meet adoration to my household gods,
When I am gone. He works his work, I mine.

    There lies the port; the vessel puffs her sail;
There gloom the dark, broad seas. My mariners,
Souls that have toil'd, and wrought, and thought
      with me,—
That ever with a frolic welcome took
The thunder and the sunshine, and opposed
Free hearts, free foreheads,—you and I are old;
Old age hath yet his honor and his toil.
Death closes all; but something ere the end,
Some work of noble note, may yet be done,
Not unbecoming men that strove with Gods.
The lights begin to twinkle from the rocks;
The long day wanes; the slow moon climbs; the
      deep

Moans round with many voices. Come, my
       friends.
'Tis not too late to seek a newer world.
Push off, and sitting well in order smite
The sounding furrows; for my purpose holds
To sail beyond the sunset, and the baths
Of all the western stars, until I die.
It may be that the gulfs will wash us down;
It may be we shall touch the Happy Isles,
And see the great Achilles, whom we knew.
Tho' much is taken, much abides; and tho'
We are not now that strength which in old days
Moved earth and heaven, that which we are, we
       are,—
One equal temper of heroic hearts,
Made weak by time and fate, but strong in will
To strive, to seek, to find, and not to yield.

Tithonus

The woods decay, the woods decay and fall,
The vapors weep their burthen to the ground,
Man comes and tills the field and lies beneath,
And after many a summer dies the swan.
Me only cruel immortality
Consumes; I wither slowly in thine arms,
Here at the quiet limit of the world,
A white-hair'd shadow roaming like a dream
The ever-silent spaces of the East,
Far-folded mists, and gleaming halls of morn.
   Alas! for this gray shadow, once a man—
So glorious in his beauty and thy choice,
Who madest him thy chosen, that he seem'd
To his great heart none other than a God!
I ask'd thee, 'Give me immortality.'
Then didst thou grant mine asking with a smile,
Like wealthy men who care not how they give.
But thy strong Hours indignant work'd their wills,
And beat me down and marr'd and wasted me,
And tho' they could not end me, left me maim'd
To dwell in presence of immortal youth,
Immortal age beside immortal youth,
And all I was in ashes. Can thy love,
Thy beauty, make amends, tho' even now,
Close over us, the silver star, thy guide,
Shines in those tremulous eyes that fill with tears
To hear me? Let me go; take back thy gift.
Why should a man desire in any way

To vary from the kindly race of men,
Or pass beyond the goal of ordinance
Where all should pause, as is most meet for all?

   A soft air fans the cloud apart; there comes
A glimpse of that dark world where I was born.
Once more the old mysterious glimmer steals
From thy pure brows, and from thy shoulders
        pure,
And bosom beating with a heart renew'd.
Thy cheek begins to redden thro' the gloom,
Thy sweet eyes brighten slowly close to mine,
Ere yet they blind the stars, and the wild team
Which love thee, yearning for thy yoke, arise
And shake the darkness from their loosen'd
        manes,
And beat the twilight into flakes of fire.

   Lo! ever thus thou growest beautiful
In silence, then before thine answer given
Departest, and thy tears are on my cheek.

   Why wilt thou ever scare me with thy tears,
And make me tremble lest a saying learnt,
In days far-off, on that dark earth, be true?
'The Gods themselves cannot recall their gifts.'

   Ay me! ay me! with what another heart
In days far-off, and with what other eyes
I used to watch—if I be he that watch'd—
The lucid outline forming round thee; saw
The dim curls kindle into sunny rings;
Changed with thy mystic change, and felt my
        blood

Glow with the glow that slowly crimson'd all
Thy presence and thy portals, while I lay,
Mouth, forehead, eyelids, growing dewy-warm
With kisses balmier than half-opening buds
Of April, and could hear the lips that kiss'd
Whispering I knew not what of wild and sweet,
Like that strange song I heard Apollo sing,
While Ilion like a mist rose into towers.

Yet hold me not for ever in thine East;
How can my nature longer mix with thine?
Coldly thy rosy shadows bathe me, cold
Are all thy lights, and cold my wrinkled feet
Upon thy glimmering thresholds, when the steam
Floats up from those dim fields about the homes
Of happy men that have the power to die,
And grassy barrows of the happier dead.
Release me, and restore me to the ground.
Thou seest all things, thou wilt see my grave;
Thou wilt renew thy beauty morn by morn,
I earth in earth forget these empty courts,
And thee returning on thy silver wheels.

Locksley Hall

Comrades, leave me here a little, while as yet 'tis
    early morn;
Leave me here, and when you want me, sound
    upon the bugle-horn.

'Tis the place, and all around it, as of old, the
    curlews call,
Dreary gleams about the moorland flying over
    Locksley Hall;

Locksley Hall, that in the distance overlooks the
    sandy tracts,
And the hollow ocean-ridges roaring into cataracts.

Many a night from yonder ivied casement, ere I
    went to rest,
Did I look on great Orion sloping slowly to the west.

Many a night I saw the Pleiads, rising thro' the
    mellow shade,
Glitter like a swarm of fireflies tangled in a silver
    braid.

Here about the beach I wander'd, nourishing a
    youth sublime
With the fairy tales of science, and the long result
    of time;

When the centuries behind me like a fruitful land
        reposed;
When I clung to all the present for the promise
        that it closed;

When I dipt into the future far as human eye
        could see,
Saw the vision of the world and all the wonder
        that would be.—

In the spring a fuller crimson comes upon the
        robin's breast;
In the spring the wanton lapwing gets himself
        another crest;

In the spring a livelier iris changes on the
        burnish'd dove;
In the spring a young man's fancy lightly turns to
        thoughts of love.

Then her cheek was pale and thinner than should
        be for one so young,
And her eyes on all my motions with a mute
        observance hung.

And I said, 'My cousin Amy, speak, and speak the
        truth to me,
Trust me, cousin, all the current of my being sets
        to thee.'

On her pallid cheek and forehead came a color
          and a light,
As I have seen the rosy red flushing in the
          northern night.

And she turn'd—her bosom shaken with a sudden
          storm of sighs—
All the spirit deeply dawning in the dark of hazel
          eyes—

Saying, 'I have hid my feelings, fearing they
          should do me wrong;'
Saying, 'Dost thou love me, cousin?' weeping, 'I
          have loved thee long.'

Love took up the glass of Time, and turn'd it in his
          glowing hands;
Every moment, lightly shaken, ran itself in golden
          sands.

Love took up the harp of Life, and smote on all the
          chords with might;
Smote the chord of Self, that, trembling, past in
          music out of sight.

Many a morning on the moorland did we hear the
          copses ring,
And her whisper throng'd my pulses with the
          fulness of the spring.

Many an evening by the waters did we watch the
      stately ships,
And our spirits rush'd together at the touching of
      the lips.

O my cousin, shallow-hearted! O my Amy, mine
      no more!
O the dreary, dreary moorland! O the barren,
      barren shore!

Falser than all fancy fathoms, falser than all songs
      have sung,
Puppet to a father's threat, and servile to a
      shrewish tongue!

Is it well to wish thee happy?—having known
      me—to decline
On a range of lower feelings and a narrower heart
      than mine!

Yet it shall be; thou shalt lower to his level day by
      day,
What is fine within thee growing coarse to
      sympathize with clay.

As the husband is, the wife is; thou art mated with
      a clown,
And the grossness of his nature will have weight to
      drag thee down.

He will hold thee, when his passion shall have
      spent its novel force,
Something better than his dog, a little dearer than
      his horse.

What is this? his eyes are heavy; think not they are
      glazed with wine.
Go to him, it is thy duty; kiss him, take his hand
      in thine.

It may be my lord is weary, that his brain is
      overwrought;
Soothe him with thy finer fancies, touch him with
      thy lighter thought.

He will answer to the purpose, easy things to
      understand—
Better thou wert dead before me, tho' I slew thee
      with my hand!

Better thou and I were lying, hidden from the
      heart's disgrace,
Roll'd in one another's arms, and silent in a last
      embrace.

Cursed be the social wants that sin against the
      strength of youth!
Cursed be the social lies that warp us from the
      living truth!

Cursed be the sickly forms that err from honest
   Nature's rule!
Cursed be the gold that gilds the straiten'd
   forehead of the fool!

Well—'tis well that I should bluster!—Hadst thou
   less unworthy proved—
Would to God—for I had loved thee more than
   ever wife was loved.

Am I mad, that I should cherish that which bears
   but bitter fruit?
I will pluck it from my bosom, tho' my heart be at
   the root.

Never, tho' my mortal summers to such length of
   years should come
As the many-winter'd crow that leads the clanging
   rookery home.

Where is comfort? in division of the records of the
   mind?
Can I part her from herself, and love her, as I
   knew her, kind?

I remember one that perish'd; sweetly did she
   speak and move;
Such a one do I remember, whom to look at was
   to love.

Can I think of her as dead, and love her for the
  love she bore?
No—she never loved me truly; love is love for
  evermore.

Comfort? comfort scorn'd of devils! this is truth
  the poet sings,
That a sorrow's crown of sorrow is remembering
  happier things.

Drug thy memories, lest thou learn it, lest thy
  heart be put to proof,
In the dead unhappy night, and when the rain is
  on the roof.

Like a dog, he hunts in dreams, and thou art
  staring at the wall,
Where the dying night-lamp flickers, and the
  shadows rise and fall.

Then a hand shall pass before thee, pointing to his
  drunken sleep,
To thy widow'd marriage-pillows, to the tears that
  thou wilt weep.

Thou shalt hear the 'Never, never,' whisper'd by
  the phantom years,
And a song from out the distance in the ringing of
  thine ears;

And an eye shall vex thee, looking ancient
        kindness on thy pain.
Turn thee, turn thee on thy pillow; get thee to thy
        rest again.

Nay, but Nature brings thee solace; for a tender
        voice will cry.
'Tis a purer life than thine, a lip to drain thy
        trouble dry.

Baby lips will laugh me down; my latest rival
        brings thee rest.
Baby fingers, waxen touches, press me from the
        mother's breast.

O, the child too clothes the father with a dearness
        not his due.
Half is thine and half is his; it will be worthy of
        the two.

O, I see thee old and formal, fitted to thy petty part,
With a little hoard of maxims preaching down a
        daughter's heart.

'They were dangerous guides the feelings—she
        herself was not exempt—
Truly, she herself had suffer'd'—Perish in thy self-
        contempt!

Overlive it—lower yet—be happy! wherefore
     should I care?
I myself must mix with action, lest I wither by
     despair.

What is that which I should turn to, lighting upon
     days like these?
Every door is barr'd with gold, and opens but to
     golden keys.

Every gate is throng'd with suitors, all the markets
     overflow.
I have but an angry fancy; what is that which I
     should do?

I had been content to perish, falling on the
     foeman's ground,
When the ranks are roll'd in vapor, and the
     winds are laid with sound.

But the jingling of the guinea helps the hurt that
     Honor feels,
And the nations do but murmur, snarling at each
     other's heels.

Can I but relive in sadness? I will turn that earlier
     page.
Hide me from my deep emotion, O thou
     wondrous Mother-Age!

Make me feel the wild pulsation that I felt before
      the strife,
When I heard my days before me, and the tumult
      of my life;

Yearning for the large excitement that the coming
      years would yield,
Eager-hearted as a boy when first he leaves his
      father's field,

And at night along the dusky highway near and
      nearer drawn,
Sees in heaven the light of London flaring like a
      dreary dawn;

And his spirit leaps within him to be gone before
      him then,
Underneath the light he looks at, in among the
      throngs of men;

Men, my brothers, men the workers, ever reaping
      something new;
That which they have done but earnest of the
      things that they shall do.

For I dipt into the future, far as human eye could
      see,
Saw the Vision of the world, and all the wonder
      that would be;

Saw the heavens fill with commerce, argosies of
　　　　magic sails,
Pilots of the purple twilight dropping down with
　　　　costly bales;

Heard the heavens fill with shouting, and there
　　　　rain'd a ghastly dew
From the nations' airy navies grappling in the
　　　　central blue;

Far along the world-wide whisper of the south-
　　　　wind rushing warm,
With the standards of the peoples plunging thro'
　　　　the thunder-storm;

Till the war-drum throbb'd no longer, and the
　　　　battle-flags were furl'd
In the Parliament of man, the Federation of the
　　　　world.

There the common sense of most shall hold a
　　　　fretful realm in awe,
And the kindly earth shall slumber, lapt in
　　　　universal law.

So I triumph'd ere my passion sweeping thro' me
　　　　left me dry,
Left me with the palsied heart, and left me with
　　　　the jaundiced eye;

Eye, to which all order festers, all things here are
            out of joint:
Science moves, but slowly, slowly, creeping on
            from point to point:

Slowly comes a hungry people, as a lion, creeping
            nigher,
Glares at one that nods and winks behind a
            slowly-dying fire.

Yet I doubt not thro' the ages one increasing
            purpose runs,
And the thoughts of men are widen'd with the
            process of the suns.

What is that to him that reaps not harvest of his
            youthful joys,
Tho' the deep heart of existence beat for ever like a
            boy's?

Knowledge comes, but wisdom lingers, and I
            linger on the shore,
And the individual withers, and the world is more
            and more.

Knowledge comes, but wisdom lingers, and he
            bears a laden breast,
Full of sad experience, moving toward the stillness
            of his rest.

Hark, my merry comrades call me, sounding on
the bugle-horn,
They to whom my foolish passion were a target for
their scorn.

Shall it not be scorn to me to harp on such a
moulder'd string?
I am shamed thro' all my nature to have loved so
slight a thing.

Weakness to be wroth with weakness! woman's
pleasure, woman's pain—
Nature made them blinder motions bounded in a
shallower brain.

Woman is the lesser man, and all thy passions,
match'd with mine,
Are as moonlight unto sunlight, and as water unto
wine—

Here at least, where nature sickens, nothing. Ah,
for some retreat
Deep in yonder shining Orient, where my life
began to beat,

Where in wild Mahratta-battle fell my father evil-
starr'd;—
I was left a trampled orphan, and a selfish uncle's
ward.

Or to burst all links of habit—there to wander far
away,
On from island unto island at the gateways of the
day.

Larger constellations burning, mellow moons and
happy skies,
Breadths of tropic shade and palms in cluster,
knots of Paradise.

Never comes the trader, never floats an European
flag,
Slides the bird o'er lustrous woodland, swings the
trailer from the crag;

Droops the heavy-blossom'd bower, hangs the
heavy-fruited tree—
Summer isles of Eden lying in dark-purple spheres
of sea.

There methinks would be enjoyment more than in
this march of mind,
In the steamship, in the railway, in the thoughts
that shake mankind.

There the passions cramp'd no longer shall have
scope and breathing space;
I will take some savage woman, she shall rear my
dusky race.

Iron-jointed, supple-sinew'd, they shall dive, and
        they shall run,
Catch the wild goat by the hair, and hurl their
        lances in the sun;

Whistle back the parrot's call, and leap the
        rainbows of the brooks,
Not with blinded eyesight poring over miserable
        books—

Fool, again the dream, the fancy! but I *know* my
        words are wild,
But I count the gray barbarian lower than the
        Christian child.

I, to herd with narrow foreheads, vacant of our
        glorious gains,
Like a beast with lower pleasures, like a beast with
        lower pains!

Mated with a squalid savage—what to me were
        sun or clime?
I the heir of all the ages, in the foremost files of
        time—

I that rather held it better men should perish one
        by one,
Than that earth should stand at gaze like Joshua's
        moon in Ajalon!

Not in vain the distance beacons. Forward,
        forward let us range,
Let the great world spin for ever down the ringing
        grooves of change.

Thro' the shadow of the globe we sweep into the
        younger day;
Better fifty years of Europe than a cycle of Cathay.

Mother-Age,—for mine I knew not,—help me as
        when life begun;
Rift the hills, and roll the waters, flash the
        lightnings, weigh the sun.

O, I see the crescent promise of my spirit hath not
        set.
Ancient founts of inspiration well thro' all my
        fancy yet.

Howsoever these things be, a long farewell to
        Locksley Hall!
Now for me the woods may wither, now for me
        the roof-tree fall.

Comes a vapor from the margin, blackening over
        heath and holt,
Cramming all the blast before it, in its breast a
        thunderbolt.

Let it fall on Locksley Hall, with rain or hail, or
        fire or snow;
For the mighty wind arises, roaring seaward, and I
        go.

Sir Galahad

My good blade carves the casques of men,
   My tough lance thrusteth sure,
My strength is as the strength of ten,
   Because my heart is pure.
The shattering trumpet shrilleth high,
   The hard brands shiver on the steel,
The splinter'd spear-shafts crack and fly,
   The horse and rider reel;
They reel, they roll in clanging lists,
   And when the tide of combat stands,
Perfume and flowers fall in showers,
   That lightly rain from ladies' hands.

How sweet are looks that ladies bend
   On whom their favors fall!
From them I battle till the end,
   To save from shame and thrall;
But all my heart is drawn above,
   My knees are bow'd in crypt and shrine;
I never felt the kiss of love,
   Nor maiden's hand in mine.
More bounteous aspects on me beam,
   Me mightier transports move and thrill;
So keep I fair thro' faith and prayer
   A virgin heart in work and will.

When down the stormy crescent goes,
   A light before me swims,
Between dark stems the forest glows,

I hear a noise of hymns.
Then by some secret shrine I ride;
   I hear a voice, but none are there;
The stalls are void, the doors are wide,
   The tapers burning fair.
Fair gleams the snowy altar-cloth,
   The silver vessels sparkle clean,
The shrill bell rings, the censer swings,
   And solemn chaunts resound between.

Sometimes on lonely mountain-meres
   I find a magic bark.
I leap on board; no helmsman steers;
   I float till all is dark.
A gentle sound, an awful light!
   Three angels bear the Holy Grail;
With folded feet, in stoles of white,
   On sleeping wings they sail.
Ah, blessed vision! blood of God!
   My spirit beats her mortal bars,
As down dark tides the glory slides,
   And starlike mingles with the stars.

When on my goodly charger borne
   Thro' dreaming towns I go,
The cock crows ere the Christmas morn,
   The streets are dumb with snow.
The tempest crackles on the leads,
   And, ringing, springs from brand and mail;
But o'er the dark a glory spreads,
   And gilds the driving hail.

I leave the plain, I climb the height;
  No branchy thicket shelter yields;
But blessed forms in whistling storms
  Fly o'er waste fens and windy fields.

A maiden knight—to me is given
  Such hope, I know not fear;
I yearn to breathe the airs of heaven
  That often meet me here.
I muse on joy that will not cease,
  Pure spaces clothed in living beams,
Pure lilies of eternal peace,
  Whose odors haunt my dreams;
And, stricken by an angel's hand,
  This mortal armor that I wear,
This weight and size, this heart and eyes,
  Are touch'd, are turn'd to finest air.

The clouds are broken in the sky,
  And thro' the mountain-walls
A rolling organ-harmony
  Swells up and shakes and falls.
Then move the trees, the copses nod,
  Wings flutter, voices hover clear:
'O just and faithful knight of God!
  Ride on! the prize is near.'
So pass I hostel, hall, and grange;
  By bridge and ford, by park and pale,
All-arm'd I ride, whate'er betide,
  Until I find the Holy Grail.

A Farewell

Flow down, cold rivulet, to the sea,
   Thy tribute wave deliver;
No more by thee my steps shall be,
   For ever and for ever.

Flow, softly flow, by lawn and lea,
   A rivulet, then a river;
Nowhere by thee my steps shall be,
   For ever and for ever.

But here will sigh thine alder-tree,
   And here thine aspen shiver;
And here by thee will hum the bee,
   For ever and for ever.

A thousand suns will stream on thee,
   A thousand moons will quiver;
But not by thee my steps shall be,
   For ever and for ever.

'Break, Break, Break'

Break, break, break,
   On thy cold gray stones, O Sea!
And I would that my tongue could utter
   The thoughts that arise in me.

O, well for the fisherman's boy,
   That he shouts with his sister at play!
O, well for the sailor lad,
   That he sings in his boat on the bay!

And the stately ships go on
   To their haven under the hill;
But O for the touch of a vanish'd hand,
   And the sound of a voice that is still!

Break, break, break,
   At the foot of thy crags, O Sea!
But the tender grace of a day that is dead
   Will never come back to me.

'Sweet and Low'

Sweet and low, sweet and low,
   Wind of the western sea,
Low, low, breathe and blow,
   Wind of the western sea!
Over the rolling waters go,
Come from the dying moon, and blow,
   Blow him again to me;
While my little one, while my pretty one, sleeps.

Sleep and rest, sleep and rest,
   Father will come to thee soon;
Rest, rest, on mother's breast,
   Father will come to thee soon;
Father will come to his babe in the nest,
Silver sails all out of the west
   Under the silver moon;
Sleep, my little one, sleep, my pretty one, sleep.

'Tears, Idle Tears'

Tears, idle tears, I know not what they mean,
Tears from the depth of some divine despair
Rise in the heart, and gather to the eyes,
In looking on the happy autumn-fields,
And thinking of the days that are no more.

Fresh as the first beam glittering on a sail,
That brings our friends up from the underworld,
Sad as the last which reddens over one
That sinks with all we love below the verge;
So sad, so fresh, the days that are no more.

Ah, sad and strange, as in dark summer dawns
The earliest pipe of half-awaken'd birds
To dying ears, when unto dying eyes
The casement slowly grows a glimmering square;
So sad, so strange, the days that are no more.

Dear as remember'd kisses after death,
And sweet as those by hopeless fancy feign'd
On lips that are for others; deep as love,
Deep as first love, and wild with all regret;
O Death in Life, the days that are no more!

In Memoriam A.H.H.

Strong Son of God, immortal Love,
  Whom we, that have not seen thy face,
  By faith, and faith alone, embrace,
Believing where we cannot prove;

Thine are these orbs of light and shade;
  Thou madest Life in man and brute;
  Thou madest Death; and lo, thy foot
Is on the skull which thou hast made.

Thou wilt not leave us in the dust:
  Thou madest man, he knows not why,
  He thinks he was not made to die;
And thou hast made him: thou art just.

Thou seemest human and divine,
  The highest, holiest manhood, thou.
  Our wills are ours, we know not how;
Our wills are ours, to make them thine.

Our little systems have their day;
  They have their day and cease to be;
  They are but broken lights of thee,
And thou, O Lord, art more than they.

We have but faith: we cannot know,
   For knowledge is of things we see;
   And yet we trust it comes from thee,
A beam in darkness: let it grow.

Let knowledge grow from more to more,
   But more of reverence in us dwell;
   That mind and soul, according well,
May make one music as before,

But vaster. We are fools and slight;
   We mock thee when we do not fear:
   But help thy foolish ones to bear;
Help thy vain worlds to bear thy light.

Forgive what seem'd my sin in me,
   What seem'd my worth since I began;
   For merit lives from man to man,
And not from man, O Lord, to thee.

Forgive my grief for one removed,
   Thy creature, whom I found so fair.
   I trust he lives in thee, and there
I find him worthier to be loved.

Forgive these wild and wandering cries,
   Confusions of a wasted youth;
   Forgive them where they fail in truth,
And in thy wisdom make me wise.

The Charge of the Light Brigade

I

Half a league, half a league,
Half a league onward,
All in the valley of Death
  Rode the six hundred.
'Forward the Light Brigade!
Charge for the guns!' he said.
Into the valley of Death
  Rode the six hundred.

II

'Forward the Light Brigade!'
Was there a man dismay'd?
Not tho' the soldier knew
Some one had blunder'd.
Theirs not to make reply,
Theirs not to reason why,
Theirs but to do and die.
Into the valley of Death
Rode the six hundred.

III

Cannon to right of them,
Cannon to left of them,
Cannon in front of them

Volley'd and thunder'd;
Storm'd at with shot and shell,
Boldly they rode and well,
Into the jaws of Death,
Into the mouth of hell
    Rode the six hundred.

IV

Flash'd all their sabres bare,
Flash'd as they turn'd in air
Sabring the gunners there,
Charging an army, while
    All the world wonder'd.
Plunged in the battery-smoke
Right thro' the line they broke;
Cossack and Russian
Reel'd from the sabre-stroke
    Shatter'd and sunder'd.
Then they rode back, but not,
    Not the six hundred.

V

Cannon to right of them,
Cannon to left of them,
Cannon behind them
    Volley'd and thunder'd;
Storm'd at with shot and shell,
While horse and hero fell,
They that had fought so well

Came thro' the jaws of Death,
Back from the mouth of hell,
All that was left of them,
  Left of six hundred.

VI

When can their glory fade?
O the wild charge they made!
  All the world wonder'd.
Honor the charge they made!
Honor the Light Brigade,
  Noble six hundred!

Cradle Song

What does little birdie say
In her nest at peep of day?
Let me fly, says little birdie,
Mother, let me fly away.
Birdie, rest a little longer,
Till the little wings are stronger,
So she rests a little longer,
Then she flies away.

What does little baby say,
In her bed at peep of day?
Baby says, like little birdie,
Let me rise and fly away.
Baby, sleep a little longer,
Till the little limbs are stronger;
If she sleeps a little longer,
Baby too shall fly away.

Literary Squabbles

Ah God! the petty fools of rhyme
 That shriek and sweat in pigmy wars
Before the stony face of Time,
 And look'd at by the silent stars;

Who hate each other for a song,
 And do their little best to bite
And pinch their brethren in the throng,
 And scratch the very dead for spite;

And strain to make an inch of room
 For their sweet selves, and cannot hear
The sullen Lethe rolling doom
 On them and theirs and all things here;

When one small touch of Charity
 Could lift them nearer Godlike state
Than if the crowded Orb should cry
 Like those who cried Diana great.

And I too talk, and lose the touch
 I talk of. Surely, after all,
The noblest answer unto such
 Is perfect stillness when they brawl.

'Flower in the Crannied Wall'

Flower in the crannied wall,
I pluck you out of the crannies,
I hold you here, root and all, in my hand,
Little flower—but *if* I could understand
What you are, root and all, and all in all,
I should know what God and man is.

The Charge of the Heavy Brigade at Balaclava

October 25, 1854

Prologue
To General Hamley

Our birches yellowing and from each
    The light leaf falling fast,
While squirrels from our fiery beech
    Were bearing off the mast,
You came, and look'd and loved the view
    Long-known and loved by me,
Green Sussex fading into blue
    With one gray glimpse of sea;
And, gazing from this height alone,
    We spoke of what had been
Most marvellous in the wars your own
    Crimean eyes had seen;
And now—like old-world inns that take
    Some warrior for a sign
That therewithin a guest may make
    True cheer with honest wine—
Because you heard the lines I read
    Nor utter'd word of blame,
I dare without your leave to head
    These rhymings with your name,
Who know you but as one of those
    I fain would meet again,

Yet know you, as your England knows
    That you and all your men
Were soldiers to her heart's desire,
    When, in the vanish'd year,
You saw the league-long rampart-fire
    Flare from Tel-el-Kebir
Thro' darkness, and the foe was driven,
    And Wolseley overthrew
Arabi, and the stars in heaven
    Paled, and the glory grew.

The Charge

I

The charge of the gallant three hundred, the Heavy
        Brigade!
Down the hill, down the hill, thousands of
        Russians,
Thousands of horsemen, drew to the valley—and
        stay'd;
For Scarlett and Scarlett's three hundred were
        riding by
When the points of the Russian lances arose in the
        sky;
And he call'd, 'Left wheel into line!' and they
        wheel'd and obey'd.
Then he look'd at the host that had halted he
        knew not why,
And he turn'd half round, and he bade his

trumpeter sound
To the charge, and he rode on ahead, as he waved
      his blade
To the gallant three hundred whose glory will
          never die—
'Follow,' and up the hill, up the hill, up the hill,
Follow'd the Heavy Brigade.

II

The trumpet, the gallop, the charge, and the might
        of the fight!
Thousands of horsemen had gather'd there on the
        height,
With a wing push'd out to the left and a wing to
        the right,
And who shall escape if they close? but he dash'd
        up alone
Thro' the great gray slope of men,
Sway'd his sabre, and held his own
Like an Englishman there and then.
All in a moment follow'd with force
Three that were next in their fiery course,
Wedged themselves in between horse and horse,
Fought for their lives in the narrow gap they had
        made—
Four amid thousands! and up the hill, up the hill,
Gallopt the gallant three hundred, the Heavy
        Brigade.

III

Fell like a cannon-shot,
Burst like a thunderbolt,
Crash'd like a hurricane,
Broke thro' the mass from below,
Drove thro' the midst of the foe,
Plunged up and down, to and fro,
Rode flashing blow upon blow,
Brave Inniskillens and Greys
Whirling their sabres in circles of light!
And some of us, all in amaze,
Who were held for a while from the fight,
And were only standing at gaze,
When the dark-muffled Russian crowd
Folded its wings from the left and the right,
And roll'd them around like a cloud,—
O, mad for the charge and the battle were we,
When our own good redcoats sank from sight,
Like drops of blood in a dark-gray sea,
And we turn'd to each other, whispering, all
      dismay'd,
'Lost are the gallant three hundred of Scarlett's
      Brigade!'

IV

'Lost one and all' were the words
Mutter'd in our dismay;
But they rode like victors and lords

Thro' the forest of lances and swords
In the heart of the Russian hordes,
They rode, or they stood at bay—
Struck with the sword-hand and slew,
Down with the bridle-hand drew
The foe from the saddle and threw
Underfoot there in the fray—
Ranged like a storm or stood like a rock
In the wave of a stormy day;
Till suddenly shock upon shock
Stagger'd the mass from without,
Drove it in wild disarray,
For our men gallopt up with a cheer and a shout,
And the foeman surged, and waver'd, and reel'd
Up the hill, up the hill, up the hill, out of the field,
And over the brow and away.

V

Glory to each and to all, and the charge that they
       made!
Glory to all the three hundred, and all the Brigade!

NOTE.—*The 'three hundred' of the 'Heavy Brigade' who
made this famous charge were the Scots Greys and the
2d squadron of Inniskillens; the remainder of the 'Heavy
Brigade' subsequently dashing up to their support.*

    *The 'three' were Scarlett's aide-de-camp, Elliot, and
the trumpeter, and Shegog the orderly, who had been
close behind him.*

Epilogue

IRENE

Not this way will you set your name
　　A star among the stars.

POET

What way?

IRENE

　　You praise when you should blame
The barbarism of wars.
A juster epoch has begun.

POET

　　Yet tho' this cheek be gray,
And that bright hair the modern sun,
　　Those eyes the blue to-day,
You wrong me, passionate little friend.
　　I would that wars should cease,
I would the globe from end to end
　　Might sow and reap in peace,
And some new Spirit o'erbear the old,
　　Or Trade re-frain the Powers
From war with kindly links of gold,
　　Or Love with wreaths of flowers.
Slav, Teuton, Kelt, I count them all
　　My friends and brother souls,
With all the peoples, great and small,
　　That wheel between the poles.

But since our mortal shadow, Ill,
    To waste this earth began—
Perchance from some abuse of Will
    In worlds before the man
Involving ours—he needs must fight
    To make true peace his own,
He needs must combat might with might,
    Or Might would rule alone;
And who loves war for war's own sake
    Is fool, or crazed, or worse;
But let the patriot-soldier take
    His meed of fame in verse;
Nay—tho' that realm were in the wrong
    For which her warriors bleed,
It still were right to crown with song
    The warrior's noble deed—
A crown the Singer hopes may last,
    For so the deed endures;
But Song will vanish in the Vast;
    And that large phrase of yours
'A star among the stars,' my dear,
    Is girlish talk at best;
For dare we dally with the sphere
    As he did half in jest,
Old Horace? 'I will strike,' said he,
    'The stars with head sublime,'
But scarce could see, as now we see,
    The man in space and time,
So drew perchance a happier lot
    Than ours, who rhyme to-day.

The fires that arch this dusky dot—
    Yon myriad-worlded way—
The vast sun-clusters' gather'd blaze,
    World-isles in lonely skies,
Whole heavens within themselves, amaze
    Our brief humanities.
And so does Earth; for Homer's fame,
    Tho' carved in harder stone—
The falling drop will make his name
    As mortal as my own.

IRENE

No!

POET

    Let it live then—ay, till when?
    Earth passes, all is lost
In what they prophesy, our wise men,
    Sun-flame or sunless frost,
And deed and song alike are swept
    Away, and all in vain
As far as man can see, except
    The man himself remain;
And tho', in this lean age forlorn,
    Too many a voice may cry
That man can have no after-morn,
    Not yet of those am I.
The man remains, and whatsoe'er
    He wrought of good or brave
Will mould him thro' the cycle-year
    That dawns behind the grave.

And here the Singer for his art
    Not all in vain may plead
'The song that nerves a nation's heart
    Is in itself a deed.'

Locksley Hall Sixty Years After

Late, my grandson! half the morning have I paced
    these sandy tracts,
Watch'd again the hollow ridges roaring into
    cataracts,

Wander'd back to living boyhood while I heard the
    curlews call,
I myself so close on death, and death itself in
    Locksley Hall.

So—your happy suit was blasted—she the
    faultless, the divine;
And you liken—boyish babble—this boy-love of
    yours with mine.

I myself have often babbled doubtless of a foolish
    past;
Babble, babble; our old England may go down in
    babble at last.

'Curse him!' curse your fellow-victim? call him
    dotard in your rage?
Eyes that lured a doting boyhood well might fool a
    dotard's age.

Jilted for a wealthier! wealthier? yet perhaps she
    was not wise;
I remember how you kiss'd the miniature with
    those sweet eyes.

In the hall there hangs a painting—Amy's arms
        about my neck—
Happy children in a sunbeam sitting on the ribs of
        wreck.

In my life there was a picture, she that clasp'd my
        neck had flown;
I was left within the shadow sitting on the wreck
        alone.

Yours has been a slighter ailment, will you sicken
        for her sake?
You, not you! your modern amorist is of easier,
        earthlier make.

Amy loved me, Amy fail'd me, Amy was a timid
        child;
But your Judith—but your worldling—*she* had
        never driven me wild.

She that holds the diamond necklace dearer than
        the golden ring,
She that finds a winter sunset fairer than a morn of
        spring.

She that in her heart is brooding on his briefer
        lease of life,
While she vows 'till death shall part us,' she the
        would-be-widow wife.

She the worldling born of worldlings—father,
     mother—be content,
Even the homely farm can teach us there is
     something in descent.

Yonder in that chapel, slowly sinking now into the
     ground,
Lies the warrior, my forefather, with his feet upon
     the hound.

Cross'd! for once he sail'd the sea to crush the
     Moslem in his pride;
Dead the warrior, dead his glory, dead the cause in
     which he died.

Yet how often I and Amy in the mouldering aisle
     have stood,
Gazing for one pensive moment on that founder of
     our blood.

There again I stood to-day, and where of old we
     knelt in prayer,
Close beneath the casement crimson with the
     shield of Locksley—there,

All in white Italian marble, looking still as if she
     smiled,
Lies my Amy dead in childbirth, dead the mother,
     dead the child.

Dead—and sixty years ago, and dead her aged
    husband now—
I, this old white-headed dreamer, stoopt and kiss'd
    her marble brow.

Gone the fires of youth, the follies, furies, curses,
    passionate tears,
Gone like fires and floods and earthquakes of the
    planet's dawning years.

Fires that shook me once, but now to silent ashes
    fallen away.
Cold upon the dead volcano sleeps the gleam of
    dying day.

Gone the tyrant of my youth, and mute below the
    chancel stones,
All his virtues—I forgive them—black in white
    above his bones.

Gone the comrades of my bivouac, some in fight
    against the foe,
Some thro' age and slow diseases, gone as all on
    earth will go.

Gone with whom for forty years my life in golden
    sequence ran,
She with all the charm of woman, she with all the
    breadth of man,

Strong in will and rich in wisdom, Edith, yet so
      lowly-sweet,
Woman to her inmost heart, and woman to her
      tender feet,

Very woman of very woman, nurse of ailing body
      and mind,
She that link'd again the broken chain that bound
      me to my kind.

Here to-day was Amy with me, while I wander'd
      down the coast,
Near us Edith's holy shadow, smiling at the slighter
      ghost.

Gone our sailor son thy father, Leonard early lost
      at sea;
Thou alone, my boy, of Amy's kin and mine art left
      to me.

Gone thy tender-natured mother, wearying to be
      left alone,
Pining for the stronger heart that once had beat
      beside her own.

Truth, for truth is truth, he worshipt, being true
      as he was brave;
Good, for good is good, he follow'd, yet he look'd
      beyond the grave,

Wiser there than you, that crowning barren Death
       as lord of all,
Deem this over-tragic drama's closing curtain is the
       pall!

Beautiful was death in him, who saw the death,
       but kept the deck,
Saving women and their babes, and sinking with
       the sinking wreck,

Gone for ever! Ever? no—for since our dying race
       began,
Ever, ever, and for ever was the leading light of
       man.

Those that in barbarian burials kill'd the slave, and
       slew the wife
Felt within themselves the sacred passion of the
       second life.

Indian warriors dream of ampler hunting grounds
       beyond the night;
Even the black Australian dying hopes he shall
       return, a white.

Truth for truth, and good for good! The good, the
       true, the pure, the just—
Take the charm 'For ever' from them, and they
       crumble into dust.

Gone the cry of 'Forward, Forward,' lost within a
          growing gloom;
Lost, or only heard in silence from the silence of a
          tomb.

Half the marvels of my morning, triumphs over
          time and space,
Staled by frequence, shrunk by usage into
          commonest common place!

'Forward' rang the voices then, and of the many
          mine was one.
Let us hush this cry of 'Forward' till ten thousand
          years have gone.

Far among the vanish'd races, old Assyrian kings
          would flay
Captives whom they caught in battle—iron-
          hearted victors they.

Ages after, while in Asia, he that led the wild
          Moguls,
Timur built his ghastly tower of eighty thousand
          human skulls;

Then, and here in Edward's time, an age of noblest
          English names,
Christian conquerors took and flung the conquer'd
          Christian into flames.

Love your enemy, bless your haters, said the
  Greatest of the great;
Christian love among the Churches look'd the twin
  of heathen hate.

From the golden alms of Blessing man had coin'd
  himself a curse:
Rome of Cæsar, Rome of Peter, which was crueller?
  which was worse?

France had shown a light to all men, preach'd a
  Gospel, all men's good;
Celtic Demos rose a Demon, shriek'd and slaked
  the light with blood.

Hope was ever on her mountain, watching till the
  day begun—
Crown'd with sunlight—over darkness—from the
  still unrisen sun.

Have we grown at last beyond the passions of the
  primal clan?
'Kill your enemy, for you hate him,' still, 'your
  enemy' was a man.

Have we sunk below them? peasants maim the
  helpless horse, and drive
Innocent cattle under thatch, and burn the
  kindlier brutes alive.

Brutes, the brutes are not your wrongers—burnt at
      midnight, found at morn,
Twisted hard in mortal agony with their offspring,
      born-unborn,

Clinging to the silent mother! Are we devils? are
      we men?
Sweet Saint Francis of Assisi, would that he were
      here again,

He that in his Catholic wholeness used to call the
      very flowers
Sisters, brothers—and the beasts—whose pains are
      hardly less than ours!

Chaos, Cosmos! Cosmos, Chaos! who can tell how
      all will end?
Read the wide world's annals, you, and take their
      wisdom for your friend.

Hope the best, but hold the Present fatal daughter
      of the Past,
Shape your heart to front the hour, but dream not
      that the hour will last.

Ay, if dynamite and revolver leave you courage to
      be wise—
When was age so cramm'd with menace? madness?
      written, spoken lies?

Envy wears the mask of Love, and, laughing sober
      fact to scorn,
Cries to weakest as to strongest, 'Ye are equals,
      equal-born.'

Equal-born? O yes, if yonder hill be level with the
      flat.
Charm us, orator, till the lion look no larger than
      the cat,

Till the cat thro' that mirage of overheated
      language loom
Larger than the lion,—Demos end in working its
      own doom.

Russia bursts our Indian barrier, shall we fight her?
      shall we yield?
Pause! before you sound the trumpet, hear the
      voices from the field.

Those three hundred millions under one Imperial
      sceptre now,
Shall we hold them? shall we loose them? take the
      suffrage of the plow.

Nay, but these would feel and follow Truth if only
      you and you,
Rivals of realm-ruining party, when you speak
      were wholly true.

Plowmen, shepherds, have I found, and more than
        once, and still could find,
Sons of God, and kings of men in utter nobleness
        of mind,

Truthful, trustful, looking upward to the practised
        hustings-liar;
So the higher wields the lower, while the lower is
        the higher.

Here and there a cotter's babe is royal-born by
        right divine;
Here and there my lord is lower than his oxen or
        his swine.

Chaos, Cosmos! Cosmos, Chaos! once again the
        sickening game;
Freedom, free to slay herself, and dying while they
        shout her name.

Step by step we gain'd a freedom known to
        Europe, known to all;
Step by step we rose to greatness,—thro' the
        tonguesters we may fall.

You that woo the Voices—tell them 'old experience
        is a fool,'
Teach your flatter'd kings that only those who
        cannot read can rule.

Pluck the mighty from their seat, but set no meek
     ones in their place;
Pillory Wisdom in your markets, pelt your offal at
     her face.

Tumble Nature heel o'er head, and, yelling with
     the yelling street,
Set the feet above the brain and swear the brain is
     in the feet.

Bring the old dark ages back without the faith,
     without the hope,
Break the State, the Church, the Throne, and roll
     their ruins down the slope.

Authors—essayist, atheist, novelist, realist,
     rhymester, play your part,
Paint the mortal shame of nature with the living
     hues of art.

Rip your brothers' vices open, strip your own foul
     passions bare;
Down with Reticence, down with Reverence—
     forward—naked let them stare.

Feed the budding rose of boyhood with the
     drainage of your sewer;
Send the drain into the fountain, lest the stream
     should issue pure.

Set the maiden fancies wallowing in the troughs of
        Zolaism,—
Forward, forward, ay, and backward, downward
        too into the abysm!

Do your best to charm the worst, to lower the
        rising race of men;
Have we risen from out the beast, then back into
        the beast again?

Only 'dust to dust' for me that sicken at your
        lawless din,
Dust in wholesome old-world dust before the
        newer world begin.

Heated am I? you—you wonder—well, it scarce
        becomes mine age—
Patience! let the dying actor mouth his last upon
        the stage.

Cries of unprogressive dotage ere the dotard fall
        asleep?
Noises of a current narrowing, not the music of a
        deep?

Ay, for doubtless I am old, and think gray
        thoughts, for I am gray;
After all the stormy changes shall we find a
        changeless May?

After madness, after massacre, Jacobinism and
        Jacquerie,
Some diviner force to guide us thro' the days I
        shall not see?

When the schemes and all the systems, kingdoms
        and republics fall,
Something kindlier, higher, holier—all for each
        and each for all?

All the full-brain, half-brain races, led by Justice,
        Love, and Truth;
All the millions one at length with all the visions
        of my youth?

All diseases quench'd by Science, no man halt, or
        deaf, or blind;
Stronger ever born of weaker, lustier body, larger
        mind?

Earth at last a warless world, a single race, a single
        tongue—
I have seen her far away—for is not Earth as yet so
        young?—

Every tiger madness muzzled, every serpent
        passion kill'd,
Every grim ravine a garden, every blazing desert
        till'd,

Robed in universal harvest up to either pole she
      smiles,
Universal ocean softly washing all her warless
      isles.

Warless? when her tens are thousands, and her
      thousands millions, then—
All her harvest all too narrow—who can fancy
      warless men?

Warless? war will die out late then. Will it ever?
      late or soon?
Can it, till this outworn earth be dead as yon dead
      world the moon?

Dead the new astronomy calls her.—On this day
      and at this hour,
In this gap between the sandhills, whence you see
      the Locksley tower,

Here we met, our latest meeting—Amy—sixty
      years ago—
She and I—the moon was falling greenish thro' a
      rosy glow,

Just above the gateway tower, and even where you
      see her now—
Here we stood and claspt each other, swore the
      seeming-deathless vow.—

Dead, but how her living glory lights the hall, the
dune, the grass!
Yet the moonlight is the sunlight, and the sun
himself will pass.

Venus near her! smiling downward at this earthlier
earth of ours,
Closer on the sun, perhaps a world of never fading
flowers.

Hesper, whom the poet call'd the Bringer home of
all good things—
All good things may move in Hesper, perfect
peoples, perfect kings.

Hesper—Venus—were we native to that splendor
or in Mars,
We should see the globe we groan in, fairest of
their evening stars.

Could we dream of wars and carnage, craft and
madness, lust and spite,
Roaring London, raving Paris, in that point of
peaceful light?

Might we not in glancing heavenward on a star so
silver-fair,
Yearn, and clasp the hands and murmur, 'Would to
God that we were there'?

Forward, backward, backward, forward, in the
    immeasurable sea,
Sway'd by vaster ebbs and flows than can be
    known to you or me.

All the suns—are these but symbols of
    innumerable man,
Man or Mind that sees a shadow of the planner or
    the plan?

Is there evil but on earth? or pain in every peopled
    sphere?
Well, be grateful for the sounding watchword
    'Evolution' here,

Evolution ever climbing after some ideal good,
And Reversion ever dragging Evolution in the mud.

What are men that He should heed us? cried the
    king of sacred song;
Insects of an hour, that hourly work their brother
    insect wrong,

While the silent heavens roll, and suns along their
    fiery way,
All their planets whirling round them, flash a
    million miles a day.

Many an æon moulded earth before her highest,
    man, was born,

Many an æon too may pass while earth is manless
　　　　and forlorn,

Earth so huge, and yet so bounded—pools of salt,
　　　　and plots of land—
Shallow skin of green and azure—chains of
　　　　mountain, grains of sand!

Only That which made us meant us to be
　　　　mightier by and by,
Set the sphere of all the boundless heavens within
　　　　the human eye,

Sent the shadow of Himself, the boundless, thro'
　　　　the human soul;
Boundless inward in the atom, boundless
　　　　outward, in the Whole.

———————————

Here is Locksley Hall, my grandson, here the lion-
　　　　guarded gate.
Not to-night in Locksley Hall—to-morrow—you,
　　　　you come so late.

Wreck'd—your train—or all but wreck'd? a
　　　　shatter'd wheel? a vicious boy!
Good, this forward, you that preach it, is it well to
　　　　wish you joy?

Is it well that while we range with Science,
        glorying in the Time,
City children soak and blacken soul and sense in
        city slime?

There among the glooming alleys Progress halts on
        palsied feet,
Crime and hunger cast our maidens by the
        thousand on the street.

There the master scrimps his haggard sempstress
        of her daily bread,
There a single sordid attic holds the living and the
        dead.

There the smouldering fire of fever creeps across
        the rotted floor,
And the crowded couch of incest in the warrens of
        the poor.

Nay, your pardon, cry your 'Forward,' yours are
        hope and youth, but I—
Eighty winters leave the dog too lame to follow
        with the cry,

Lame and old, and past his time, and passing now
        into the night;
Yet I would the rising race were half as eager for
        the light.

Light the fading gleam of even? light the glimmer
of the dawn?
Aged eyes may take the growing glimmer for the
gleam withdrawn.

Far away beyond her myriad coming changes earth
will be
Something other than the wildest modern guess of
you and me.

Earth may reach her earthly-worst, or if she gain
her earthly-best,
Would she find her human offspring this ideal
man at rest?

Forward then, but still remember how the course
of Time will swerve,
Crook and turn upon itself in many a backward
streaming curve.

Not the Hall to-night, my grandson! Death and
Silence hold their own.
Leave the master in the first dark hour of his last
sleep alone.

Worthier soul was he than I am, sound and
honest, rustic Squire,
Kindly landlord, boon companion—youthful
jealousy is a liar.

Cast the poison from your bosom, oust the
       madness from your brain.
Let the trampled serpent show you that you have
       not lived in vain.

Youthful! youth and age are scholars yet but in the
       lower school,
Nor is he the wisest man who never proved
       himself a fool.

Yonder lies our young sea-village—Art and Grace
       are less and less:
Science grows and Beauty dwindles—roofs of
       slated hideousness!

There is one old hostel left us where they swing
       the Locksley shield,
Till the peasant cow shall butt the 'lion passant'
       from his field.

Poor old Heraldry, poor old History, poor old
       Poetry, passing hence,
In the common deluge drowning old political
       common-sense!

Poor old voice of eighty crying after voices that
       have fled!
All I loved are vanish'd voices, all my steps are on
       the dead.

All the world is ghost to me, and as the phantom
        disappears,
Forward far and far from here is all the hope of
        eighty years.

———————————

In this hostel—I remember—I repent it o'er his
        grave—
Like a clown—by chance he met me—I refused
        the hand he gave.

From that casement where the trailer mantles all
        the mouldering bricks—
I was then in early boyhood, Edith but a child of
        six—

While I shelter'd in this archway from a day of
        driving showers—
Peept the winsome face of Edith like a flower
        among the flowers.

Here to-night! the Hall to-morrow, when they toll
        the chapel bell!
Shall I hear in one dark room a wailing, 'I have
        loved thee well'?

Then a peal that shakes the portal—one has come
        to claim his bride,
Her that shrank, and put me from her, shriek'd,
        and started from my side—

Silent echoes! You, my Leonard, use and not abuse
your day,
Move among your people, know them, follow him
who led the way,

Strove for sixty widow'd years to help his homelier
brother men,
Served the poor, and built the cottage, raised the
school, and drain'd the fen.

Hears he now the voice that wrong'd him? who
shall swear it cannot be?
Earth would never touch her worst, were one in
fifty such as he.

Ere she gain her heavenly-best, a God must
mingle with the game.
Nay, there may be those about us whom we
neither see nor name,

Felt within us as ourselves, the Powers of Good,
the Powers of Ill,
Strowing balm, or shedding poison in the
fountains of the will.

Follow you the star that lights a desert pathway,
yours or mine.
Forward, till you see the Highest Human Nature is
divine.

Follow Light, and do the Right—for man can half-
      control his doom—
Till you find the deathless Angel seated in the
      vacant tomb.

Forward, let the stormy moment fly and mingle
      with the past.
I that loathed, have come to love him. Love will
      conquer at the last.

Gone at eighty, mine own age, and I and you will
      bear the pall;
Then I leave thee lord and master, latest lord of
      Locksley Hall.

The Snowdrop

Many, many welcomes,
February fair-maid,
Ever as of old time,
Solitary firstling,
Coming in the cold time,
Prophet of the gay time,
Prophet of the May time,
Prophet of the roses,
Many, many welcomes,
February fair-maid!

Crossing the Bar

Sunset and evening star,
   And one clear call for me!
And may there be no moaning of the bar,
   When I put out to sea,

But such a tide as moving seems asleep,
   Too full for sound and foam,
When that which drew from out the boundless deep
   Turns again home.

Twilight and evening bell,
   And after that the dark!
And may there be no sadness of farewell,
   When I embark;

For tho' from out our bourne of Time and Place
   The flood may bear me far,
I hope to see my Pilot face to face
   When I have crost the bar.